Best wishes
Bob & Deb Truitt

COLLECTIBLE

BOHEMIAN

VOL. II

GLASS

1915 - 1945

ROBERT & DEBORAH TRUITT

Published by
B&D GLASS
5120 White Flint Drive
Kensington, MD 20895

Additional copies of this book may be ordered from the authors.
Price: $39.95

Other books by Robert and Deborah Truitt:

Mary Gregory Glassware, 1880-1990,
copyright 1992, second printing 1998. ($19.95)

Collectible Bohemian Glass, 1880-1940,
copyright 1995 ($49.95)

All prices include postage.

Printed by IMAGE GRAPHICS, INC. Paducah, Kentucky

In Memoriam

Ladislav Jindra
May 1907–April 1997

Historian, Humanitarian, Friend

TABLE OF CONTENTS

INTRODUCTION

This book is meant to be a companion to and a continuation of *Collectible Bohemian Glass 1880-1940*. That book primarily deals with the numerous refineries and exporters of glassware and the history of the Bohemian glass industry. This book concentrates more on the development of the glass and its various styles.

By limiting ourselves to the years 1915 to 1945, we can focus on a particular aspect of Bohemian glass which encompasses both the past and the future. The formation of an entirely new country with an established manufacturing infrastructure gave rise to opportunities that had been previously unthinkable. The birth of the Republic of Czechoslovakia on October 28, 1918 created a foundation upon which a leaner, more cohesive and profitable glass industry could be raised. Despite a shortage of raw material, inflation, and a considerable loss of foreign customers, the industry forged ahead.

Naturally, those firms that dominated the pre-war industry were the first to regain their footing. Loetz, Harrach, Kralik, Pallme-König, Rückl and Riedel had the necessary capital and resources to sustain their quality production and reestablish their foreign trade. In 1922, the Moser firm merged with Meyr's Neffe and became one of the largest manufacturing and refining companies.

In the short span of 21 years (1918-1939) the reborn Bohemian glass industry captured the hearts and pocketbooks of the world. The historical and romantic value of the glass produced during that period may never again be equaled. Therefore, we will try to give the reader the information necessary to recognize the glass and know its relevance in history.

We have concentrated on the glass made between 1915 and 1945 but in order to present a complete picture, we have gone back as far as 1910. One must remember that several designs were kept in production for many years.

The caption for each photo includes a date which indicates when that particular glass was most popular—such as, the 1920s or 1930s. Occasionally a specific date is given, if appropriate.

ACKNOWLEDGMENTS

Modern day historians have expended a great deal of effort on the glass produced between 1915 and 1945 and have documented nearly every aspect of the industry. Their efforts involved countless hours of searching through government and company records, catalogs and work books, glass collections, and wherever else their research led them. Finally, they organized their material and presented it in the form of books and magazine articles for the benefit of everyone unable to do the original research.

We have made extensive use of their writings and wish to thank them all for making the material available. It isn't possible to give credit to everyone from whom we have learned, but we must acknowledge a few of the most prolific writers.

To –

> Dr. Alena Adlerová, Torsten Bröhan,
> Antonin Langhamer, Dr. Jan Mergl,
> Dr. Duňa Panenková, Dr. Helmut Ricke
>
> – thank you for your work.

The Glass Museum in Passau, Germany has funded numerous research projects and made possible the publication of several books on Bohemian glass.

Over the years, the Moser Company has made a great deal of information available about the firm, including a comprehensive book published in 1997.

Dr. Waltraud Neuwirth at the Austrian Museum of Applied Art (ÖMAK) in Vienna has contributed greatly to the world's knowledge of Czech/Bohemian glass.

In addition to these writers and sponsors, we have received direct assistance from numerous firms and individuals.

◆ Dr. Jürgen Fischer's auction company (Heilbronn, Germany) supplied photos of hard-to-find glass.

◆ Dr. Helena Braunová, Director of the Glass Museum in Kamenický Šenov, allowed us to photograph pieces from the museum's collection.

◆   Mrs. Jaroslava Slabá, Director of the Museum of Glass and Jewelry in Jablonec, provided us with information about the Brychta figurines and allowed us to photograph several pieces owned by the museum.

◆   The District Museum in Česka Lipá allowed us to photograph several pieces in their collection.

◆   Mrs. Eva Ranšová, Director of the Glass Museum in Nový Bor, answered countless questions and made the museum's collection available to us.

Throughout the Czech Republic and Germany, the children of the refiners mentioned in this book shared with us their family histories and provided us with numerous details not available from any published source.

Here in the U.S. we were befriended by many collectors, dealers, and historians who opened their collections to us.

As always, the Rakow Library in Corning, New York provided assistance and reference material that would otherwise have made accurate research impossible.

As in the case of *Collectible Bohemian Glass 1880-1940*, this book represents the work of many people and we wish to thank everyone who helped to make it possible.

UNDERSTANDING BOHEMIAN GLASS

Professor Josef Drahoňovský spoke to the Second International Glass Congress in 1936 in London. He began his talk with these words:

"Who wants to love Bohemian glass, he must understand it, get acquainted with it, and comprehend it."

Many people collect Bohemian glass for its obvious beauty and complexity. They search it out, buy it and take it home. They put it on a shelf and admire it. Admire it, yes, but not love it. For they seldom make a real attempt to understand it. Sixty years later, we might reverse Drahoňovský's statement and say: Those who would understand Bohemian glass, must first love it.

Factual information about Bohemian glass is hard to come by. Unless you have a deep and genuine love for the glass, the complexity of gathering information will overwhelm you. If you can read the Czech language, you will have an advantage, but books and journal articles are scarce and hard to come by. Books and magazine articles written in the German language are more abundant, but they are usually quite expensive and few Americans can read German.

Information is hard to come by, but not impossible. Quite a few good books published in English have become available in the past few years. Anyone who wants to can build an adequate library which will greatly enhance the pleasure of collecting.

Understanding Bohemian glass also requires an adjustment in thinking. Reason and logic are important factors in glass collecting, but many aspects of the Bohemian glass industry will seem to be totally unreasonable or illogical to the novice collector.

One fact that presents itself early, is that the Bohemian glass industry is the product of over six centuries of tradition. Since the end of the 14th century, Bohemian glass makers were able to create just about every type of contemporary glass product. The very nature and culture of the early glass men was such that innovation and competition came naturally and soon the glass makers were contributing new formulas and techniques of their own. By 1915 every aspect of research, training, and execution had been honed to perfection.

The creation of the Republic of Czechoslovakia (from the former Austro-Hungarian lands) freed the glass industry from outside legislation and financial control. More importantly, it supplied a new source of inspiration. The Czech and Slovak cultures, long ignored, gained recognition and influence especially as consumers. The production of colored glass had long been the main-stay of the glass industry, but the new country wanted brighter colors — red, yellow, black and orange — colors that bespoke of their national costumes and taste.

The creation of a new glass school in Železný Brod primarily for the training of Czech students, resulted in an outpouring of new designs based upon Czech and Slovak ethnicity and resulted in a variety of new opportunities for the glass industry. Not only did the Czechs love the new glass — the whole world loved it.

The glass exporters had in place a highly efficient system for surviving every change in world fashion. Sometimes they created the change and other times they responded to it. The "Roaring Twenties" seems to have challenged designers and refineries to create more fanciful, inspiring and lustful designs. Judging by the number of liquor sets and decanters offered, it would seem that a glass company could support itself wholly by the sales of items related just to drinking.

The new designs were not all fun and frolic however; several companies continued to produce luxury glass. Refineries such as Schappel, Goldberg, Oertel, and Eiselt pressured the Glass Schools for new designs and the schools responded with what was called at the time: the North Bohemian style. After the Exposition International des Arts Decoratifs et Industriels Modernes in Paris in 1925, this style became known as Art Deco.

The 1920s were an exciting decade in Bohemian glass history. Moser introduced numerous broad-facet designs in exciting new colors, as well as its acid-etched friezes featuring Amazon warriors and jungle animals. Loetz expanded its Tango line of brightly colored, decorative glass. Kralik produced an outstanding line of baskets, vases, and bowls in brightly colored and tasteful designs.

All in all, it is easy to love the Bohemian glass of the 1920s and 1930s, but if you have some understanding of how it came to be, your enjoyment will increase proportionately.

MEASURES OF SUCCESS

While Bohemia was a possession of Austria, it fit neatly into a well organized system of manufacturing, importing, and exporting. At the end of World War I, the new Republic of Czechoslovakia found that it would have to fend for itself in a new world market.

Fortunately Czechoslovakia did not share the devastation suffered by many European countries during the war. Export records show respectable exports into other countries while those countries struggled to revive their own glass industries. This can best be shown with the following table.

EXPORTS FROM CZECHOSLOVAKIA
The numbers indicate the value in millions of Czech crowns
(in 1920, 1 Crown = $.01; in 1930, 1 Crown = $.03)

Exports to	1920	1924	1930
Germany	381	88	42
Austria	240	59	50
Italy	226	64	70
U.S.A.	213	323	144
Great Britain	201	198	211
France	183	66	75

From 1919 to 1923, a large percentage of the Czech exports consisted of architectural and laboratory glass used to repair war damage. By 1924 that market was about satiated and thus the major decline on the continent.

Czechoslovakia was not the only country that depended upon a strong glass industry. As central European producers rebuilt, they regained their dominance in the manufacture of glass for export. By the end of the decade Germany again led the world in glass exports with the equivalent of 2,000 million Crowns. Second was Belgium with 1,420 million Crowns, and third was Czechoslovakia with 1,375 million Crowns. This was no small accomplishment as the competing European countries rebuilt their industries with new modern factories and the Czechs made do with their pre-war facilities.

The worldwide depression of the early 1930s spared no one. Numerous small producers disappeared in the wake of declining sales. From 1929 to 1934, the production of hollow glass fell 62%, table glass was off by 38% and glass for jewelry was down 48%. Only pressed glass production managed to maintain its former numbers.

Monetary value alone is not the best criterion for measuring success. The direct competition with other countries at the numerous expositions show that the Bohemian technology, design and execution were consistently judged among the best.

At the Paris Exposition in 1925, Czechoslovakia was second only to France in total medals won, primarily due to the glass industry. The Paris Exposition was made to order for the Czechs. The emerging Art Deco style coincided perfectly with the emerging Czech ethnicity. Grand prizes and gold medals were awarded to designers and producers with names like: Horejc, Drahoňovský, Smrčková, Metelák, and Přenosil, and to the new Czech Glass School in Železný Brod.

This outpouring of new talent, combined with long-standing savvy and competence of the glass schools in Nový Bor and Kamenický Šenov, plus the elite architects from Prague and Vienna, put Czechoslovakia at the front of the design/technology race.

When the World Exhibition opened in Brussels in 1935, the Czech pavilion was dominated by glass. Thirty-eight firms attended and, as in Paris, garnered numerous awards including at least 10 grand prizes, 6 gold medals, and numerous silver medals and diplomas of honor. The 1920s and '30s were certainly a double-decade that can rival any period for the proliferation of the glass arts.

Since its founding in 1864, the firm Carl Hosch consistently displayed the newest fashions in glass design at the numerous exhibitions throughout the world. The Hosch firm was one of the largest refining-exporting companies in Bohemia, producing all types of glassware and chandeliers. Some of the numerous medals won by the Hosch firm are shown at the left.

The tradition of father-to-son training was established long before the first glass school opened in 1856. The children born to a painter were very likely to become painters as adults. The same applied to all the glass refining arts. Occasionally an exception would occur; however, by-and-large most children followed the family trade. If a youth wished to enter a vocation other than his father's, he entered into an apprenticeship which typically began with sweeping and washing. A year or more might pass without ever touching a tool of the trade, except to clean it.

After 400 years of this manner of training, coupled with the human desire to associate with neighbors having similar interests, areas of Bohemia became effectively parceled as the source of a particular type of refining. The town of Okrouhlá (near Nový Bor) was known for its painters working with gold. As early as 1820, Buquoy in South Bohemia shipped his black and red hyalith to Okrouhlá to be painted. Nový Bor is closely associated with high enamel and stained glass. Kamenický Šenov is best known for its engravers. Harrachov was home to many artists specializing in the old German manner of refinement. The area around Jablonec is known for its bead and jewelry work, and most of the 20th century pressed glass came from that same area. Glass cutters were an exception; they usually settled near the glass factories that employed them or supplied their blanks.

Quite often Bohemian glass is sold with only an area designated as its point of origin. Thus, it is helpful to the collector to be able to confirm such claims.

Nový Bor painter, Oskar Winkler, sat at the same workbench that his father used in the early 1900s. Both father and son specialized in white high enamel painting. Oskar's son, Heinz, is also a painter who works in the art department of Crystalex.

Stone wheel cutting of glass provided employment for thousands of artisans in Bohemia, not counting the manufacture of countless raw glass blanks. Early in the century Meyr's Neffe in the south, and Harrach in the north maintained large cutting shops attached to their glass factories and produced brilliant cut glass equal to the world's finest. Unfortunately their works were very rarely marked and are mostly known by catalogs and working drawings.

In the *Encyclopedia of Glass*, Phoebe Phillips gives high praise to the cut glass of Christian Dorflinger when she writes "... it was considered at one time to make the best crystal in the United States, good enough to match that of all but the best Bohemian craftsmen."

Even the cut glass of the 1920s and 1930s is rarely marked with a company name. If it is marked at all, it is probably marked "Czechoslovakia" although an occasional piece turns up with a paper company label.

The preference of the artisans involved in cutting strongly favored working at home or in small shops. The proliferation of refineries and exporters along with the wide-spread availability of electric power had a measured effect upon glass cutting. Designers could not keep up with the demands of the refineries. Many large companies (such as Hosch, Palda, and Goldberg) continued to produce designs that were popular in the first quarter of the century. The use of overlay glass (usually red, green or blue cut to clear) contributed a new look to some old patterns.

The more modern Deco designs came from the Glass Schools, Artel and Devitstil in Prague, the Wiener Werkstätte, and a sundry of Viennese and German artists. The most progressive firms were always under pressure to create new designs for a world hungry for the newest craze.

The major glass factories accounted for the majority of the sales, both for export and for the interior market. Riedel was probably best known for its superb transparent colored glass, cut in ways that blended with its modern forms. Harrach was known for complexity; Rückl for its cut-to-clear designs and the designs of Ludvika Smrčková; and Meyr's Neffe for its stemware.

Most prolific of all was Moser at Karlovy Vary. Moser employed the best designers in Czechoslovakia, Austria, and Germany to create new art forms. Leo Moser, who had been the firm's artistic director prior to assuming the directorship of the company, also contributed numerous new patterns. Although best known for its broad-facet cutting, the firm also produced numerous plastic designs by Heinrich Hussmann and Vera Lišková.

CUT GLASS

Cutting was often used in combination with stained or painted decorations. In this book, we have arranged things by their most prominent decoration type. Therefore, glassware that has been cut, can also be found in combination with other forms of refining.

Multi-layered Glass

Early in the 19th century, the Bohemian glass makers devised a process for making multi-layered glass of contrasting colors. The refineries, in turn, transformed the blanks into marvelous works of art. In the 1850s, the engravers A.H. Pfeiffer (Karlovy Vary) and Karl Pfohl (Kamenický Šenov) produced exquisite designs by engraving through a colored outer layer to a clear under layer. In the 1870s, Harrach used precise cutting in the designs of its two- and three-colored glass.

A century later, the refineries were still producing extraordinary decorations drawn from their 100 plus years of experience. By 1915, the multi-layered glass was commonly known as overlay or cased glass. Generally speaking, if the outer layer is left intact, it is usually called cased glass; if the outer layer is cut, by some means, to reveal the inner layer(s), it is called overlay glass.

Several methods were employed to penetrate the outer layer(s) of the glass. The most common methods were: cutting, engraving, acid-etching, and sand-blasting. Although the refineries continued to provide glassware based on Biedermeier and Neo-Classical designs, the emerging Art Deco style dominated the thinking at the glass schools and of the independent designers.

Artel and Devitstil (Cubism group) in Prague and the Wiener Werkstätte in Vienna began to produce the Art Deco motifs around 1908 and, by 1918 had almost abandoned all previous designs. After 1918, the majority of Viennese designs were executed by painters working on single layer glass or colored glass with a clear overlay. Only a small percent of the new designs called for cutting or engraving. The last of the great cameo designs by Beckert, Bolek and Hoffmann practically disappeared with the onset of World War I. Many of the northern cutters found work replicating Biedermeier tumblers and mantle lusters – a practice which will certainly be continued well into the 21st century.

Another style of multi-layered glass cutting that enjoyed popularity in the 1920s and 1930s was Lištované (loosely translated as border or panel glass). Developed in the workshop of Franz Heide in Česká Kamenice around 1902, Lištované went on to become a favorite of Harrach and Jílek Brothers.

Cameo glass is a form of overlay glass that is distinct even while not fitting a precise definition. The words used to describe cameo glass production are the same that describe several other forms of multi-layered glass refining. Typically (but not always) cameo glass relies on a light colored under layer, overlaid with one, two or three layers of darker colored glass. An acid resisting material is painted on the outer layer, then carefully removed to allow the acid to attack the glass and etch a pattern into the unprotected surface. The process can be repeated several times, resulting in various densities of the colored layers. When the acid etching process is finally finished, the design might be touched up by an engraver. In the case of the newer, commercial cameo, enamels might be used to add detail instead of engraving and repeated acid baths.

Cameo glass produced during the Art Nouveau period was clearly dominated by the French. The firms of Gallé, Daum Bros., and Crystaleri de Pantine produced three and four color glass of amazing complexity that was immensely popular at the time and, now (a hundred years later) continues to be some of the most sought-after glass ever produced.

Bohemian firms also made quality cameo glass during the first decade of the twentieth century, most notably Riedel, Harrach, Kralik, and Loetz. By and large, however, the Bohemian firms concentrated on iridized, painted, cut and engraved glass.

By the mid-twenties, cameo glass production was again on the rise — not the exquisite three or four color types, with intricate designs and extensive hand finishing — but simpler two and sometimes three color designs that required little or no hand work. This type became known as commercial cameo and was often produced for foreign customers and marked with names such as Richard, Velez, and Lucidus (all made by Loetz) and D'Aurys and Soleil (made by Kralik). Sometimes the object would have no signature at all, only the paper label of the firm selling the glass. Loetz cameo glass meant for the American market was usually signed (in cameo): C.a.Loetz, although no one has been able to discover the meaning of the C.a.

Colored overlay glass, cut to clear, has become some of the most sought-after glass produced during the years 1910 to 1945. The Glass Schools, plus numerous independent designers turned out countless variations on the "cut to clear" theme. The firms of Schappel, Oertel, and Meltzer gained the leading reputation for this type of decoration, although all of the major refineries offered similar wares. The Wiener Werkstätte and Artel were also proponents of "cut to clear" designs. The designers Otto Prutscher and Josef Rosipal are best remembered for their designs of this type.

In the early 1930s, Professor Drahoňovský began experimenting with a variation of two and three layered glass that featured an unusually high relief and had a rough final appearance. Drahoňovský spent the last 6 years of his life working on these designs, but never accomplished exactly what he envisioned.

In this chapter on "Cut Glass" you will find examples of a variety of techniques used to penetrate the surface of a blank -- wheel cut, acid etched, sand blasted, and others.

CUTTING AND ENGRAVING TECHNIQUES

The wheels used for cutting range in size from dime-size to 3-feet in diameter, and are made from a variety of natural or synthetic stones. Water, mixed with a grinding medium (such as graphite), is dripped on the stone and produces the cut. The wheels must be kept perfectly round and individually shaped to produce the desired cut. Large wheels, powered by water and driven by a series of pullies and belts, are mounted in a frame. The smaller wheels (usually up to 14" in diameter) are mounted on the same type of lathe used for engraving.

The wheels used for engraving are made of copper or from the same stones used for cutting wheels. Engraving wheels typically vary in size from pencil point to about 8 inches in diameter. Engraving uses the same liquids as glass cutting. Stone wheel engraving is a shallow, almost scratched, penetration; while copper wheel engraving produces deep and highly detailed motifs.

One obvious difference in the procedure is that the engraver (left photo) holds the object below or behind the wheel and can see exactly how the wheel touches the glass. The cutter (right photo) must hold the glass between her and the wheel. When the glass is covered with a black slurry of graphite, water and oil, the cutter is relying mostly on a sense of feel, rather than on sight.

$$\begin{array}{c|c} \multicolumn{2}{c}{1 - 2} \\ \hline \multicolumn{2}{c}{3 - 5} \\ \hline 6 & 7 - 8 \end{array}$$

1-2: Candlesticks. Clear lead glass. Palda. Mid-1930s. 2½".

3-5: Decanter and glasses. Clear lead glass. Palda. Paper label. Mid-1930s. 10¼"; 3½".

6: Decanter. Clear lead glass. Palda. Paper label. Mid-1930s. 6½".

7-8: Candlesticks. Clear lead glass. Palda. Mid-1930s. 9¾".

All from the collection of Elaine Palda Swiler.

Page 11:
Four pages from a Palda catalog used around 1935, to commemorate Palda's 50th anniversary.

PALDA GLASS

Albert Palda was born in Cleveland, Ohio in 1888. He was the nephew of the glass exporter/refiner Karl Palda of Nový Bor. In the mid-1930s, Karl Palda shipped several crates of glass to his nephew in the hope that Albert could wholesale it in the Cleveland area. The shipment contained all luxury glass, for which there was a very limited market. Unable to sell the glass, Albert packed it away and eventually used it in his home or as gifts. A fire in 1954 severely depleted the collection and what remained was passed on to Elaine Palda Swiler in 1984. Ms. Swiler has maintained the collection ever since and has done considerable research about the firm's roots in Bohemia.

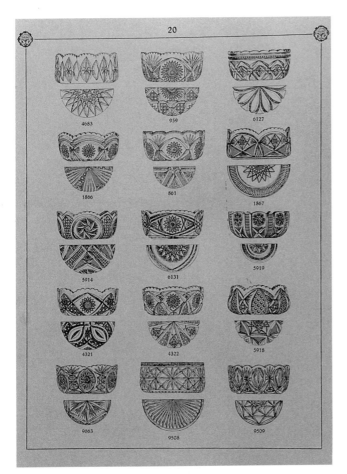

20

21

23

24

Service Nr. 5012

Page 12:
*Two pages from a Palda
catalog, used around 1933.*

Page 13:
*Two pages from a supplement
to a Gebrüder Zahn catalog,
used in 1931.*

4806/9"
9452

5016/10"
9053

5064/12"
9543

5016/10"
9443

4807
9452

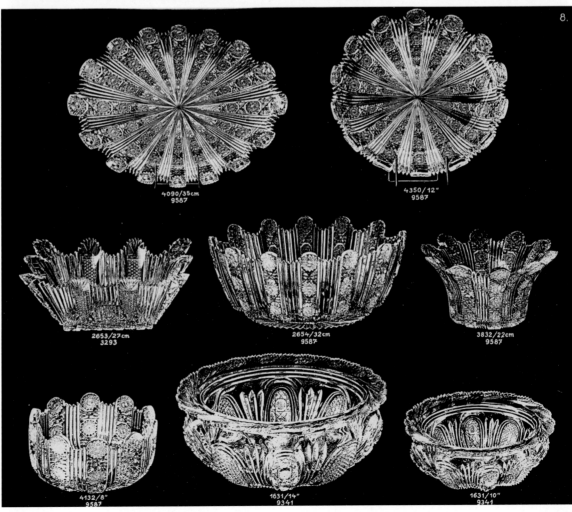

8.

4090/35cm
9587

4350/12"
9587

2653/27cm
3293

2654/32cm
9587

3832/22cm
9587

4132/8"
9587

1631/14"
9341

1631/10"
9341

1 - 3	
4 - 6	
7 - 9	10-12

1-2: *Decanter and glasses. Clear glass. Cut. Black enamel. Mid-1930s. 9¼"; 3".*

4-6: *Decanter and glasses. Clear glass. Cut and engraved. Black enamel. Mid-1930s. 10½"; 2½". Acid mark on glasses: TCHECO-SLOVAQUIE.*

7-9: *Decanter and glasses. Clear glass with red stain. Mid-1930s. 8"; 2¼".*

10-12: *Decanter and glasses. Clear glass. Cut. Black enamel. Mid-1930s. 9"; 2½".*

All from the collection of Eric Sirulnik.

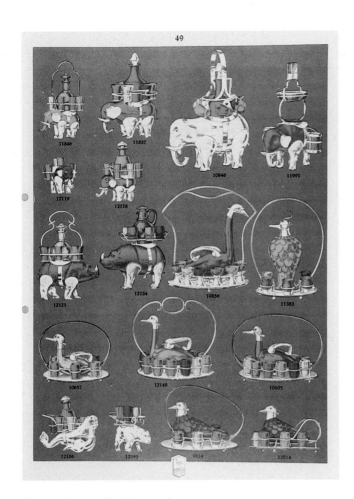

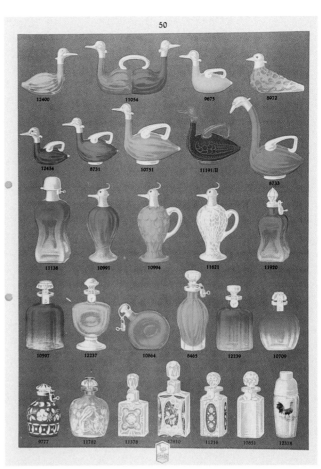

Pages from a Palda catalog used in the mid-1930s. The number of decanter and liquor sets produced by Palda alone is extraordinary.

Pages from a Palda catalog, printed in 1935 to commemorate Palda's 50th anniversary.

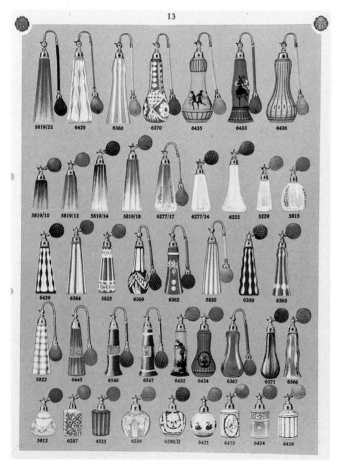

```
       1 - 3
       4 - 6
   7 | 8 - 10
```

1: *Perfume. Black enamel. Mid-1930s. 4¼".*
Collection: Eric Sirulnik.

2: *Perfume. Black enamel. Mid-1930s. 4½".*
Collection: Eric Sirulnik.

3: *Perfume. Black and red enamel. Mid-1930s. 4¼".*
Collection: Eric Sirulnik.

4: *Perfume. Black enamel. Mid-1930s. 3¼".*
Collection: Eric Sirulnik.

5: *Perfume. Black enamel. Mid-1930s. 5½".*
Collection: Eric Sirulnik.

6: *Perfume. Black enamel with gilt decoration. Mid-1930s. 3½".*
Collection: Eric Sirulnik.

7: *Dresser Box. Blue, cut to clear. Painted. 1920s-30s. 2½"H; 6"D.*
Collection: Carol and John Kelly.

8: *Perfume. Black enamel. Mid-1930s. 6¾".*
Collection: Eric Sirulnik.

9: *Perfume. Black enamel. Mid-1930s. 6¾".*
Collection: Eric Sirulnik.

10: *Perfume. Black enamel. Mid-1930s. 4". Paper label for Rudolf Mehr.*
Collection: Eric Sirulnik.

METAL FITTINGS

Atomizers and other metal fittings were mostly procured from the firm Rachmann in Nový Bor. Rachmann's foundry produced metal parts for various refineries, as well as for their own use.

1
—
2-3
4 | 5-7

1: *Palda catalog. 1935. 50th anniversary edition.*

2: *Glass. Red stain, cut to clear. Engraved, with gold fill. Late-1920s – mid-1930s. 5".*
Collection: Carol and John Kelly.

3: *Wine glass. Clear glass, stained red. Cut, engraved with gold fill. Late-1920s – mid-1930s. 9½".*
Collection: Carol and John Kelly.

4: *Glass. White, cut to blue. Painted, gilt. Late-1920s – mid-1930s. 6".*
Collection: Glass Museum Nový Bor.

5: *Glass. White, cut to green. Painted. Late-1920s – mid-1930s. 5".*
Collection: Carol and John Kelly.

6: *Glass. Pink over white, cut to clear. Painted, gilt. Late-1920s – mid-1930s. 5".*
Collection: Carol and John Kelly.

7: *Glass. Blue-green, cut to clear. Painted, gilt. Late-1920s – mid-1930s. 5".*
Collection: Carol and John Kelly.

	1	2
	3 - 5	
6	7	8

1: *Lištované footed glass. Clear glass, blue panels; engraved between panels; gilt. Palda. Mid-1930s. 6".*
Collection: Elaine Palda Swiler

2: *Footed glass. Clear glass with red, green and blue enamel; gilt. Palda. Mid-1930s. 7".*
Collection: Elaine Palda Swiler.

3: *Lištované tumbler. Clear glass, orange stained panels; gilt. Mid-1930s. 7".*
Collection: Carol and John Kelly.

4: *Lištované footed glass. Clear glass, orange stained panels; gilt. Mid-1930s. 8¾".*
Collection: Carol and John Kelly.

5: *Lištované bowl. Clear glass, orange stained panels; gilt. Mid-1930s. 4¾"D.*
Collection: Carol and John Kelly.

6: *Footed glass. Amber overlay, cut to clear. Engraved. Palda. Mid-1930s. 5¼".*
Collection: Elaine Palda Swiler.

7: *Footed glass. Clear glass, amber stem and foot. Bowl is clear with amber stain. Engraved. Palda. Mid-1930s. 6½".*
Collection: Elaine Palda Swiler.

8: *Lištované footed glass. Clear glass, green panel. Engraved between panels, with gilt. Palda. Mid-1930s. 6½".*
Collection: Elaine Palda Swiler.

1	2
3	4
5 - 6	7

All the glass on this page was designed by Alexander Pfohl, Jr.

1: Vase. Blue (also available in red, amethyst, and crystal). Josephinenhütte. 1923-28. 9".

2: Vase. Blue (also available in red, amethyst, and crystal). Josephinenhütte. 1923-28. 6½".

3: Covered bowl. Orange-amber. 1920s. 5½".

4: Footed vase. Amber. Designed for C. Wünsch. 1928-1932. 11".

5: Footed vase. Smoke. Josephinenhütte. 1923-5. 4"

6: Bowl. Smoke. Josephinenhütte. 1923-5. 4½".

7: Vase. Light green. Designed for Hantich. 1940. 6¼".

All from the collection of Walter and Brigitte Herrmann.

This type of cutting is called Profile or Broad Facet Cutting.

$$\frac{1}{\frac{2}{3}}$$

1: Bowl. Clear crystal. Design is "Cristalla" by J. Šulaka. Mid-1930s. 5¼".

Collection: Glass Museum Nový Bor.

2: Jardiniere. Uranium glass. Traditional cutting. Designed by Antonin Janak. Mid-1930s. 5".

Collection: District Museum Česká Lípa.

3: Jardiniere. Amber glass. Art Deco style cutting. Late 1920s - early 1930s. 4¾".

Collection: District Museum Česká Lípa.

1
2
3 | 4

1: Vase. Clear glass with black
    enamel; silver. Cut in the Art
    Deco style. Mid-1930s. 9".
    Collection: Eric Sirulnik.

2: Compote. Dark amethyst.
    Alternating panels have an acid
    cut frieze; other panels are
    painted with polished gold.
    Designed by Glass School
    Nový Bor. 1920s-1930s. 6¾".
    Collection: Glass Museum Nový Bor.

3: Compote. Clear glass with
    amber stem and foot. Bowl is
    cut; stained yellow and painted
    with blue transparent enamel.
    The blue panels are engraved
    and the yellow have an olive
    cut. 1920s-30s. 6¾"H; 7¼"D.
    Collection: Private.

4: Vase. Gold ruby and clear.
    Designed by Alexander Pfohl,
    Jr. for Josephinenhütte. 1926.
    5½".
    Collection: Walter and Brigitte
    Herrmann.

```
  1 | 2
  ─────
  3 - 4
─────────
5 | 6 - 7
```

1: *Vase. Red, cut to clear. Designed by Glass School Nový Bor for Meltzer. ≈1915. 7".*
   Collection: Bernd Lienemann.

2: *Stoppered bottle. Red, cut to clear. Designed by Glass School Nový Bor for Meltzer. ≈1915. 9".*
   Collection: Bernd Lienemann.

3: *Vase. Black over white, cut to clear. Karl Schappel. "Borussia." 1915-1920. 5½".*
   Collection: Bernd Lienemann.

4: *Bowl. Black over white, cut to clear. Karl Schappel. "Borussia." 1913-20. 3½"H.*
   Collection: Bernd Lienemann.

5: *Covered jar. Red, cut to clear. Probably Meltzer. 1920-25. 9".*
   Collection: Glass Museum Nový Bor .

6: *Bowl. Gold ruby, cut to clear. Designed by Alexander Pfohl, Jr. for Josephinenhütte. 1920. 3½".*
   Collection: Walter and Brigitte Herrmann.

7: *Footed glass. Red, cut to clear. Designed by Alexander Pfohl, Jr. for Josephinenhütte. 1920. 5".*
   Collection: Walter and Brigitte Herrmann.

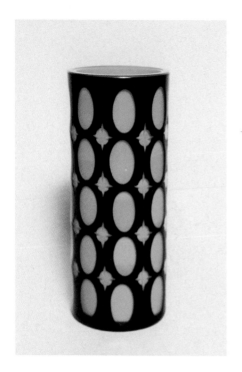

1 | 2
3 - 5
6 | 7 | 8

1: Vase. Black, cut to yellow. Oertel. ≈1915. 7½".
Collection: Bernd Lienemann.

2: Vase. Black over green, cut to clear. Paper label: Glass School Haida. 1914-20. 10½".
Collection: Bernd Lienemann.

3: Covered box. Amethyst, cut to clear. Carl Meltzer. 1914-20. 3".
Collection: Bernd Lienemann.

4: Dish. Amethyst, cut to clear. Carl Meltzer. 1914-20. 1¼".
Collection: Bernd Lienemann

5: Covered jar. Amethyst, cut to clear. Carl Meltzer. 1914-20. 5½".
Collection: Bernd Lienemann.

6: Vase. Black, cut to lavender. Oertel. 1914-20. 4".
Collection: Private.

7: Vase. Clear glass. Cut; red stain; etched flower design. Appears in catalogs from both Palda and Wünsch. Mid-1930s. 7".
Collection: Private.

8: Vase. Blue over white, cut to clear. 1918-25. 5¾".
Collection: Ken Donmoyer.

1: *Vase. Black over white, cut to clear. 1915-25. 10".*
Collection: Glass Museum Nový Bor.

2: *Stoppered bottle. Blue, cut to clear, with galvano-silver. Meltzer. 1915-20. 14½".*
Collection: Oertel Museum.

3: *Vase. Purple, cut to clear. Beyermann & Co.; probably designed by the Glass School Nový Bor. 1915-20. 10½".*
Collection: Bernd Lienemann.

4: *Vase. Red, cut to clear. Oertel. Designed by the Glass School Nový Bor. 1915-20. 8¾".*
Collection: Oertel Museum.

5: *Bowl. Blue, cut to clear. Oertel. Acid stamp: Ö. 1915-20. 3¼".*
Collection: Bernd Lienemann.

6: *Bowl. Red, cut to clear. Josephinenhütte. Designed by Alexander Pfohl, Jr. 1918. 3"H; 8¼"D.*
Collection: Walter and Brigitte Herrmann.

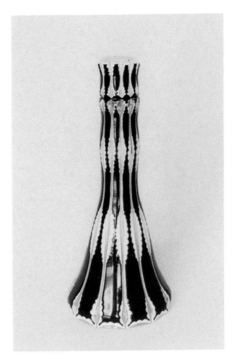

3000-3500

1500-1800

1	2
3	4
5	6-7

1: *Vase. Cameo, blue over white. Loetz (product #4635). Signed in cameo: C.a. Loetz. 1922-25. 14".*
Photo: Chrysler Museum.

2: *Vase. Cameo, brown over light green. Loetz (product #4645; decoration #G34 beech nuts and leaves). Signed in cameo: C.a. Loetz. 1922-25. 7".*
Collection: Private.

3: *Vase. Cameo, light rose background with dark rose Clematis design. Loetz. Signed in cameo: Veles. 1922-25. 9".*
Collection: Private.

VELES

4: *Vase. Cameo, blue-black over orange. Loetz. Signed in cameo: Veles. 1922-25. 11¼".*
Collection: Private.

5: *Vase. Cameo, black over orange over yellow. Loetz. Signed in cameo: Richard. 1922-25. 10".*
Photo: Jürgen Fischer.

6: *Vase. Cameo, black over clear over yellow/orange . Loetz. Signed in cameo: Richard. ≈1925. 4½".*
Collection: Private.

7: *Vase. Cameo, dark blue over red. Loetz. Signed in cameo: Richard. 1922-25. 8".*
Collection: Private.

1200-1400

NAMES ON CAMEO

Loetz made glass for various foreign companies according to their demands. The most often encountered names appearing on Loetz cameo are: Richard, Veles, Velez, and Lucidus. Loetz cameo destined for America was oftened signed: C.a.Loetz.

Kralik also produced cameo with French-sounding names, such as: D'Aurys and Soleil.

$$\frac{\dfrac{1}{2}}{3 \mid 4 \mid 5\text{-}6}$$

1: Bowl. Cameo, lavender over white. Designed by Marey Beckert-Schider for Loetz. ≈1924. 4"H; 7¾"D.
Collection: Private.

2: Bowl. Cameo, 4 colors: light blue with clear, coral and dark red overlay. Black glass feet. Loetz. 1924-25. 5".
Collection: Passau Glass Museum.

3: Vase. Cameo, light green with clear and dark brown overlay. Loetz. Product #1839. ≈1925. 11".
Collection: Passau Glass Museum.

4: Vase. Cameo, light rose with clear and dark violet overlay. Loetz. ≈1922-25. 7".
Collection: Passau Glass Museum.

5. Footed vase. Cameo, red over uranium glass; acid etched decoration. Loetz. 1923. 6¾".
Photo: Jürgen Fischer.

6. Vase. Cameo, red over uranium glass; acid etched decoration. Loetz. 1923. 10½".
Photo: Jürgen Fischer.

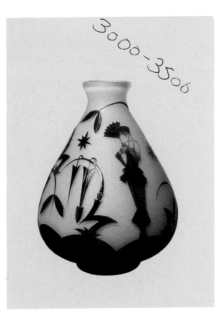

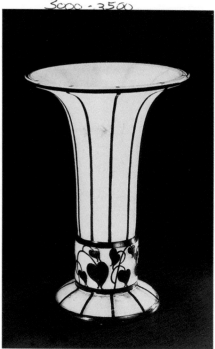

1	2
3	4
5	6

1: *Vase. White medallions over yellow; cut to clear; black enamel. Designed by Glass School Nový Bor. 1915-25. 10½".*

Collection: Glass Museum Nový Bor.

2: *Vase. Pink over white, cut to clear; green and gold enamel. Designed by Glass School Kamenický Šenov. Paper label: St.St. Signed in gold: WB. 1915-20. 6¼".*

Collection: Glass Museum Kamenický Šenov.

3: *Vase. Clear glass inside, layered with white and black. Design is acid etched. Designed by Hans Bolek for Loetz. 1915. 8".*

Photo: Jürgen Fischer.

4: *Footed vase. Light olive green over yellow, with black enamel. Loetz. 1924-25. 7¼".*

Photo: Jürgen Fischer.

5: *Desk lamp. Cameo shade on metal base. Emeralite #7. 1930s. Shade is 2¼"H; 7½"W.*

Collection: Joe Mattis.

6: *Vase. Light green over yellow, with black enamel. Designed by Marey Beckert-Schider for Loetz. 1924-25. 4¼".*

Collection: Bernd Lienemann.

$$\frac{1 \mid 2}{3 - 5}$$
$$\overline{6 - 8}$$

1: Covered vase. Cobalt blue; cut; acid etched bands of polished gold. Moser. ≈1920. 16".

Collection: Passau Glass Museum.

2: Covered urn. Violet amethyst glass. Cut, with frieze depicting Amazon warriors in battle. Moser. 1925. 13½".

Collection: Private.

3: Vase. Amber glass with stylistic frieze. Moser. ≈1925. 6".

Photo: Jürgen Fischer.

4: Stoppered bottle. Amber glass with frieze of Amazon warriors. Moser. ≈1925. 9".

Photo: Jürgen Fischer.

5: Footed vase. Cobalt blue glass with "Masque" frieze. Moser. ≈ 1925. 5¾"

Photo: Jürgen Fischer.

6: Vase. Dark red over uranium glass; cut; gold trim; with elephant frieze. Designed by Rudolf Wels for Moser, as part of the "Animor" series. ≈1925. 9½".

Photo: Jürgen Fischer.

7: Vase. Cobalt blue, with elephant frieze. Designed by Rudolf Wels for Moser, as part of the "Animor" series. ≈1925. 13¾".

Photo: Jürgen Fischer.

8: Vase. Black glass with stork design in gold. Designed by Rudolf Wels for Moser. ≈1925. 9½".

Photo: Jürgen Fischer.

1
———
2
———
3 | 4

1: *Vase. Cameo; violet-brown over rose over clear. Signed in cameo: Moser Karlsbad and LMK. 1911-25. 4¾".*
Collection: Bernd Lienemann.

2: *Vase. Acid etched in relief and painted with polished gold. Designed by Rudolf Wels for Moser.≈1925. 6".*
Collection: Passau Glass Museum.

3: *Vase. Green glass; acid cut, and engraved. Designed by Heinrich Hussmann for Moser. ≈1925. 10".*
Collection: Passau Glass Museum.

4: *Vase. Amber glass; acid cut and engraved. Designed by Heinrich Hussmann for Moser. ≈1925. 9½".*
Collection: Private.

Heinrich Hussmann's designs for the deeply etched vases allowed the acid to find its own path once it passed the resist painted on the surface. This produced a very irregular pattern.

1000 -1400

```
      1
    2 3
  4 5 6
```

1: Vase. Brown glass over clear; acid etched, cut and air brushed with brown enamel. Designed by Prof. Foltas, Nový Bor. 1930. 6½".
Photo: Jürgen Fischer.

2: Vase. Coral red over clear over white opal glass; with black enamel. Designed by Marey Beckert-Schider for Loetz. Product #2296. 1925. 7½".
Collection: Passau Glass Museum.

3: Vase. Cobalt blue over clear over white opal glass; with black enamel. Loetz. Product #2167. 1925. 6".
Collection: Passau Glass Museum.

4: Vase. Green glass with acid etched medallion. Loetz. ≈1925. 7".
Collection: Passau Glass Museum.

5: Vase. White over unpolished clear glass. Sandblasted design. J. Schreiber and Neffen. 1920-25. 7½".
Collection: Private.

6: Vase. Dark rose glass. Acid etched, with gold background. Oertel. Product #2692. 1920-25. 6½".
Collection: Glass Museum Nový Bor .

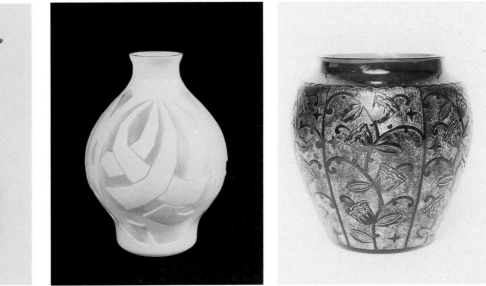

Copper wheel engraving, as we know it today, dates back to the year 1588. In that year Casper Lehmann received the imperial privilege of providing glassware to the Austrian crown. It is believed that Lehmann alone possessed the ability to create wheel engravings.

Slowly the art spread and was improved. New glass formulas were devised to provide a more perfect vehicle for engraving and, for nearly 50 years, copper wheel engraving was the sole provenance of Bohemian artisans. Emigrating Bohemian craftsmen carried their abilities to every corner of Europe and in time to the world.

By the 20th century, the center of glass engraving had moved from Prague to the village of Kamenický Šenov. The Glass School established in Kamenický Šenov in March 1856 engaged the finest engravers as professors and designers. By 1918, Kamenický Šenov was a virtual hot bed of engravers, producing everything from mundane dresser boxes to exquisite neo-classical masterpieces.

The Art Deco years brought a revolution in motifs to the engraving industry. The new Glass School in Železný Brod and the Academy of Applied Art in Prague encouraged the emergence of the Czech culture in art. In any discussion about engraved Czech glass of the 1920s and '30s, two names dominate: Jaroslav Horejc and Josef Drahoňovský.

Jaroslav Horejc (pronounced Hor-eights) designed and helped engrave a bold new form of figural engraving that influenced both Czech and German engraving. Four cups designed by Horejc won a grand prize for J.&L. Lobmeyr's Neffe Stefan Rath at the Paris Exposition in 1925.

Josef Drahoňovský (see pages 37 through 45) created thousands of designs which emphasized the nude figure in such natural settings that the figures appeared sensuous without being sexual.

The studio engravers, Max Rössler and Ladislav Přenosil, were among the best of a long list of highly skilled artisans.

Despite the ever changing economic conditions and stylistic swings of the 20th century, engraved glass has maintained its niche in glass refining.

If the background glass is removed and the design is raised above the surface, it is termed **cameo engraving**.

If the design is cut into the surface, it is termed **intaglio engraving**.

ENGRAVED GLASS

  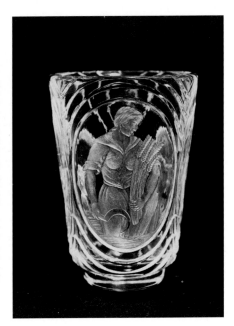

1	2	3
4	5	6

1,2,3:　*Three views of a cup designed and produced at the Glass School in Kamenický Šenov. Ethnic motifs like these dominated the art after the creation of Czechoslovakia in 1918. Paper label: Made in Czechoslovakia. Engraved initials: R.K. (possibly Rufin Koppel). Early 1920s. 6".*

Collection: Glass Museum Kamenický Šenov.

4,5,6:　*Cameo design produced by acid etching and copper wheel engraving. Glass School in Kamenický Šenov. Early 1920s. 12¼".*

Collection: Glass Museum Kamenický Šenov.

  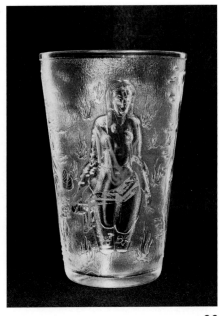

1	2
3	4
5	6

1-4: Four sides of a vase depicting (1) winter, (2) spring, (3) summer, and (4) fall. Designed by Alexander Pfohl, Jr. in 1929. The vase was cut in 1929 but not engraved until 1990 when Pfohl's daughter acquired it and engaged Franz Zinke to do the engraving. 12½".

Collection: Walter and Brigitte Herrmann.

5: Clear vase with allegory of music. Designed by Alexander Pfohl, Jr. in 1936. Engraved by Rudolf Weisel. 13".

Collection: Walter and Brigitte Herrmann.

6: Clear vase with allegory of the earth. Designed by Alexander Pfohl, Jr. in 1936. Engraved by Rudolf Weisel. 12½".

Photo: Jürgen Fischer.

```
   | 1
 2 | 3
 4 | 5
```

1: Commercially produced, engraved vase, of good quality. Acid marked: Czechoslovakia. Late 1930s. 7¼".

Collection: Private.

2: Beaker. Engraved by Max Rössler. The "S" pattern, top and bottom, is cameo engraved; the two lions (the emblem of Czechoslovakia) are intaglio engraved. The medallion is blank. ≈1920. 5½".

Photo: Jürgen Fischer.

3: Beaker. Designed by Michael Powolny. Engraved by Max Rössler. 1920. 5".

Photo: Jürgen Fischer.

4: Covered box. Part of a 5-piece dresser set. 1915-20. 2".

Collection: Glass Museum Kamenický Šenov.

5: Vase. Cut, engraved, and diamond stippled. Designed by Prof. A. Dorn. Engraved by a student. 1934. 5¾".

Collection: Glass Museum Kamenický Šenov.

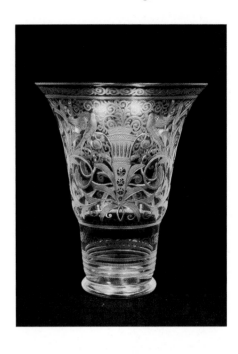

1500 - 2000

Two clear beakers and two views of a clear vase, designed and engraved by Heinrich Pech. 1936-1940.
Photos provided by Walter Pech.

2500 - 3000

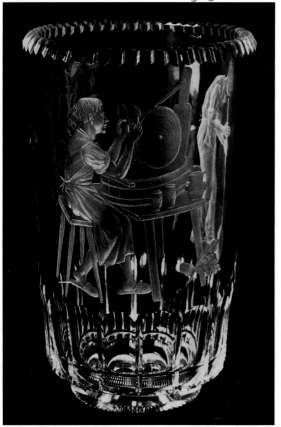
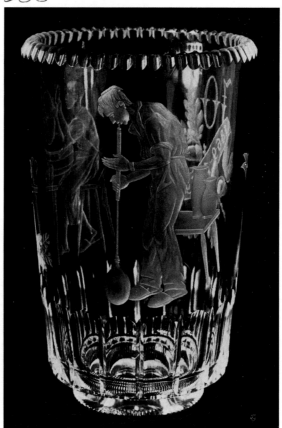

JOSEF DRAHOŇOVSKÝ

ALL
3,000 -5000

A NOTE ABOUT DRAHOŇOVSKÝ

In this book, the glass is more or less arranged by decorating technique, with only a small amount of information about the people and companies that produced it. This is in contrast with the format for *Collectible Bohemian Glass, 1880-1940,* which presented a brief history of individuals and companies, followed by photos of the glassware they produced. In the case of Drahoňovský, we must make an exception. The life and contributions of Drahoňovský are unknown to most Americans and we have a rare opportunity to publish photos of his work.

The photos appearing in this book were made in Prague in the early 1930s by a studio photographer to illustrate two books by Dr. Jindřich Čadík about the works of Drahoňovský and his students: *Josef Drahoňovský, Sochař a Glyptik* and *Dílo Josefa Drahoňovského.* These original photos are now in the possession of an American art dealer and he has graciously allowed us to reprint them here. Some have never been printed and many will never be printed again.

If any one person deserves the title of "The Father of Modern Czech Glass" it would very likely be Professor Josef Drahoňovský. The life works of Drahoňovský appear as a one-man shock wave through the world of Czech cultural and applied arts. Not only did he apply his hand to all of the major art forms, he ascended to the pinnacle of each field -- drawing, painting, architecture, sculpture, design, and engraving, and most important of all, a professor of remarkable inspirational ability. Many of his students became professors at the Academy of Applied Art in Prague or at the Železný Brod Glass School and in turn passed on his philosophy to the most renowned studio artists, designers and professors of contemporary Czech glass.

Born in Volavec, near Turnov, on March 27,1877, into a middle class, agricultural family, Drahoňovský exhibited a keen aptitude for the arts. At age 13, he was accepted at the Industrial Art School in Turnov to learn stone cutting (precious and semiprecious stone) from Karl Zapp. Upon graduation at age 17, Drahoňovský moved to Vienna where he worked for Dorflinger for two years. During that time, he made extensive use of the numerous museums and cultural exhibits available to hone his interest in Hellenistic and Renaissance art.

At age 19, Drahoňovský returned to Prague and entered the Academy of Applied Arts, studying under Celda Klouček and Stanislav Sucharda. Drahoňovský would remain associated with the Academy until his death on July 20, 1938.

Glyptic. Carved in rock crystal. Set as a pendant.

In 1904, Drahoňovský officially became Sucharda's assistant and from 1908 to 1911 he held the designation "Assistant Teacher." In 1911 he replaced Sucharda as the head of the general school. The Academy suspended operations during World War I and, when it reopened in 1918, he became the Director of the Special Sculptural Department, replacing Klouček. Drahoňovský's students received a well-rounded education in the various art disciplines pertaining to the creation of sculptural works.

Drahoňovský augmented his income from the Academy by producing countless sculptural works of art in various media: clay, marble, bronze, and plaster. In addition to his three dimensional works, he produced medals, diplomas, and plaques.

During the time that the school was closed, Drahoňovský returned to his roots as a stone cutter and glyptic artist. Drahoňovský chose smoky topaz and rock crystal for most of his glyptic works. To merely say that Drahoňovský was prolific would be a gross understatement.

Finally, at the age of 44, Drahoňovský turned his attention to engraved glass. In September 1921, he arranged with the Jílek Brothers Glassworks in Kamenický Šenov to supply him with overlay glass. Drahoňovský began with red over clear and blue over clear for his first efforts. His technique was similar to that used by Franz Zach and Karl Pfohl in the 1850s. His motifs, however, were based upon Czech nationalist and patriotic images.

1| 2

1: Vase. Red over clear. "Harvest under the Kozákov." Designed by Josef Drahoňovský. After 1921. 10".

Collection: A. Van Dam.

2: Vase. Blue over clear. Designed by Josef Drahoňovský. After 1921. 10".

Collection: A. Van Dam.

Up to that point, the Academy of Applied Art did not offer training in the glass arts per se, but Drahoňovský's knowledge in modeling, sculpture, and composition attracted students from all disciplines. By 1922 the school was offering studio training to both glyptic artists and glass engravers. The glyptic students mostly came from Turnov and the engravers came from the glass schools — František Pazourek and Oswald Lippert from Kamenický Šenov, Artur Plewa from Nový Bor, and Alois Hásek from Železný Brod. Drahoňovský and his students prepared a display for the 1925 Paris exhibition that impressed the judges and influenced the design of engraved glass through the Art Deco period. Goblets and covered vases reflected his love for both simplicity and completeness. Each vessel was perfectly cut and polished to accentuate and complement the engraving.

Throughout the 1920s and until his death on July 20, 1938, Drahoňovský created prizes, awards and gifts for the Czech government. Perhaps his most famous piece was the St. Wenceslaus vase presented to Pope Pius XI in 1929.

After the 1925 exhibition, Drahoňovský's studio accelerated its emphasis on engraving. Students were still drilled in the fundamentals, but the students were clearly there to learn engraving. Out of necessity, Drahoňovský was forced to create designs that his students could copy on a material less costly than the beakers and vases that he had been using. During the school year 1930-31, Drahoňovský created several plaques engraved on flat glass. The plaques featured from one to four pieces of glass engraved on one or both sides. Many of Drahoňovský's originals were set on a base made of pure rock crystal; others were set on a glass or painted wooden base.

St. Wenceslaus vase presented to Pope Pius XI in 1929. Designed by Josef Drahoňovský. 22½".

In 1932, Drahoňovský again turned to the Jílek Brothers Glassworks as a source of two-colored glass, white over black for deep cameo-like relief engraving. Evidently he was not happy with the results and switched to blue glass with a thick white overlay and a thin red layer in between for effect. Drahoňovský worked closely with his old student and friend, Karel Tuček to realize his new designs. Students were also given the opportunity to experiment with new cutting methods which would satisfy Drahoňovský's vision of a new, modern art form. Several cups and small vases were produced in this manner, but they didn't catch on with the public and Drahoňovský died before he could complete his experiments.

Drahoňovský is remembered as one of the great demagogues of the 20th century.

Page 41:

1	2
3	4

1: *Small covered vase, carved from solid rock crystal. Late 1920s. 8".*
Collection: A. Van Dam.

2: *Covered Ear-of-Corn vase. Depicts a version of "The Harvest." 1925. 17".*
Collection: A. Van Dam.

3: *Six-sided vase. "The Vintage." Late 1920s. 10".*
Collection: A. Van Dam.

4: *Six-sided vase. "Morning, Midday, Evening." Late 1920s. 10".*
Collection: A. Van Dam.

Vase at left: ≈1925. 10".
Design drawing at right.
Collection: A. Van Dam.

Drahoňovský popularized the form of the inverted bell shaped glass in the mid-1920s. His designs were meticulous and included every detail.

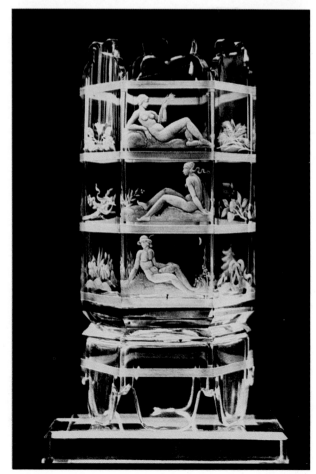

3000 – 5000

GLYPTICS

Webster's *New Collegiate Dictionary* describes glyptics as "a carved figure: hence a pictograph representing a form for sculpture." Harlon Newman's *An Illustrated Dictionary of Glass* defines glyptics as "susceptible to carving, especially hard stones and gems, but also applicable to certain types of glass…"

Drahoňovský designed and, along with his students, produced thousands of small glyptic art works from a variety of materials — rock crystal, glass, topaz, smoky quartz, and other semi-precious stones. Some of the designs were used on perfume bottle stoppers. Many of the glyptic motifs are also found on vases and plaques. One of Drahoňovský's best pupils, František Pazourek, became a leading designer for Heinrich Hoffmann in Jablonec.

Page 42:

1	2
3	4

1: *Vase. "Spring is Coming, the Earth Awakes, Winter is Going Away." Mid-1920s. 10½".*

2: *Vase. "Magic Garden." Late-1920s.*

3: *Vase. "On the Brook." Won a Grand Prize in Barcelona, 1929. 10".*

4: *Vase. "Diana." Won a Diploma of Honor in Paris, 1925. 10".*

All from the collection of A. Van Dam.

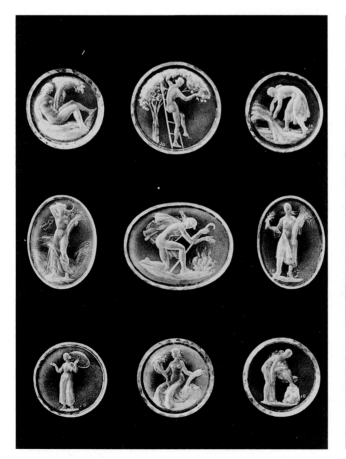

ALL 3000-5000

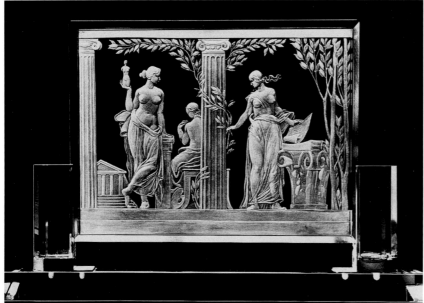

Page 44:

1
2
3

1: Plaque. "Morning." After 1930. ≈12" wide.

2: Plaque. "Art, Science, and Architecture." After 1930. ≈13" wide.

3: Plaque. "Enchanted Garden." Engraved by Bohmil Vele. After 1930. ≈13" wide.

These plaques are mounted on pure, rock crystal bases.

Page 45:

1	2
3	4
5	6

1: Plaque. "Orpheus Playing to the Animals." Engraved by Karel Tuček. After 1930. ≈13" wide. 3 sections.

2: Plaque. "Mid-Day." After 1930. ≈12" wide.

3: Plaque. "Thor." After 1930. ≈13" wide. 3 sections.

4: Plaque. "Music and Poetry." After 1930. ≈12" wide.

5: Plaque. "The Coming of Spring." After 1930. ≈13" wide. 3 sections.

6: Drawing of the engraving "The Coming of Spring."

All from the collection of A. Van Dam.

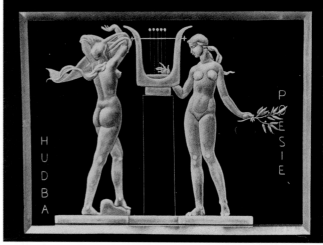

For centuries the cold glass refining techniques of the Romans and Babylonians lay forgotten and it was left to the glass blowers to make their products as decorative as they would ever be. Some forms of decoration helped to make the glass easier to hold (such as prunts on an ale glass); others, such as external ribbing, made it more impact-resistant. Some of the decoration, as found on the Venetian-inspired glass, was purely decorative.

By 1915, the Bohemian glass blowers had mastered every conceivable form of hot glass decoration. Artists and glass designers relied on the ability of the glass blowers to execute their demanding and complicated concepts.

The ever-changing economic conditions strongly influenced the percentage of refined glass being produced. One must remember that refining existed as a completely separate branch of the glass industry. Although many glass manufacturers operated their own refineries, the majority of refined glass was produced by small companies who bought blanks from various glass houses. Transportation to and from the refinery, breakage, and the refiner's labor accounted for 60 to 70% of the wholesale price.

Without a doubt the most abundant type of furnace decorated glassware produced during the 1920s and 1930s was what we now call spatter-ware. Although the patterns appear to be haphazard at first glance, they actually required great precision in the layout and marvering stage of the blowing process. Many of the patterns were used on a variety of table articles and remained in production for several years; therefore a candlestick made in 1930 can perfectly match a bowl or vase made in 1935.

Second place in proliferation goes to the mono-colored glass with contrasting embellishments. First exhibited by Loetz at Cologne, Germany in 1914, it was put aside until the end of World War I. By 1920, Loetz revived the designs, as did many other Bohemian and Bavarian glass makers. Loetz referred to its brightly colored line as "Tango"—a name that has stayed with it until this day. Other firms also used the Tango designation for their production. So popular has this glass become that, regardless of who manufactured it, it is generally referred to as Tango.

In addition to the Tango line developed by Loetz, the firm relied on the highly developed skills of its glass makers to produce variations of its famous Art Nouveau lines. The outstanding iridescence produced at Klášterský Mlýn added considerably to vessels that would otherwise be considered quite average.

FURNACE DECORATED GLASS

Crackle glass, made by rapid surface chilling with water, was especially popular in the 1920s and '30s. Another attractive technique involved the introduction of air bubbles which created a distinct appearance in the finished object.

Throughout the 1920s and 1930s the search for new colors and glass formulas reached an all-time high. Chemists and designers worked hand-in-hand to integrate new shapes that would take advantage of the new formulas. The revival of Venetian glass styles married to Art Deco colors inspired much of the Czech glass produced in the late 1920s.

The vast majority of the glass shown in this section was designed in the early to mid-1920s. It was kept in constant production for many years. We have simplified the dating by using the 1930s decade for most of the glassware shown.

The method of glass blowing in Bohemia traditionally involves the use of wooden molds, split and hinged with provisions at the top of the mold to accommodate an "over blow." After the item is annealed, the over blow is cracked off, and the top ground flat and polished.

If the object has to be opened and shaped by the maker (such as in the making of a pitcher), the object would most likely be transferred to a snap, rather than to a pontil rod. Holding the object in a snap eliminates the need to grind off the pontil scar.

1-5: *Vases. Mono-colored glass with black hot glass windings. #4 is cased white and yellow glass. 1930s. Sizes range from 4½" to 11".*

Collection: Charles and Barbara Plummer.

6-8: *Vases. Mono-colored glass with black hot glass windings. Left and middle are marked: Made in Czechoslovakia. 1930s. 8½"; 8½"; 9¼".*

Collection: Kevin P. Inman.

9-13: *Vases. Mono-colored and variegated glass with blue hot glass windings. Middle vase is marked: Czecho-Slovakia. 1930s. Sizes range from 5¼" to 8¾".*

Collection: Kevin P. Inman.

The Venetian influence on Bohemian glassware of the 1920s and 1930s is apparent in much of the glassware in this section. We have included a generous number of photos so the collector can discriminate between Bohemian glass and the glass produced in other countries, most notably Italy. All of the glassware shown in this section is marked or is known to be a Bohemian product.

$$\frac{\begin{matrix} 1 - 2 \\ 3 - 5 \end{matrix}}{6 - 9}$$

1-2: Vases. Multi-colored glass with blue hot glass windings. 1930s. 12".
 Collection: Kevin P. Inman.

3-5: Vases. Mono-colored glass with blue hot glass windings. 1930s. 9"; 9½"; 9".
 Collection: Kevin P. Inman.

6-9: Vases. Colored glass with black hot glass windings in the form of a serpent. #6 and #9 have spatter-glass at the base. 1930s. 8"; 6½"; 6½"; 8¼".
 Collection: Kevin P. Inman.

```
 1 - 2
 3 - 4
 5 | 6 | 7
```

1-2: Vases. Horn shape. Clear glass with colored glass machine threading. Marked: Czecho-Slovakia. 1930s. 7".
Collection: Joe Mattis.

3: Fan vase. Orange glass with spatter pattern on base. 1930s. 10½".
Collection: Kevin P. Inman.

4: Fan vase. Light green glass with blue glass threading on top. 1930s. 7¾".
Collection: Kevin P. Inman.

5: Pitcher. Clear glass with blue and green overlay extending from bottom to top; with blue glass threading on top. Acid marked: Czechoslovakia. 1930s. 10".
Collection: Joe Mattis.

6: Vase. Clear glass with red overlay extending from bottom to top; blue glass threading on top; blown to size after the threading was applied. Marked: Czechoslovakia. 1930s. 10¼".
Collection: Kevin P. Inman.

7: Vase. Orange glass with yellow glass threading; blown to size after the threading was applied. 1930s. 6½".
Collection: Joe Mattis.

$$\frac{\begin{array}{cc} 1 & - & 2 \end{array}}{\begin{array}{c|c} 3 & - & 4 \\ \hline 5 & 6 & - & 7 \end{array}}$$

1: *Pedestal bowl. Green glass with blue hot glass windings, prunts, and base. 1930s. 5¼".*

Collection: Kevin P. Inman.

2: *Vase. Orange glass with black hot glass windings and prunts. 1930s. 8".*

Collection: Kevin P. Inman.

3: *Vase. Red glass with black hot glass windings and prunts. 1930s. 9½".*

Collection: Joe Mattis.

4: *Vase. Red glass with black hot glass windings. Marked: Czecho-Slovakia. 1930s. 8¼".*

Collection: Joe Mattis.

1, 2, 3, and 4 were most likely made by Loetz.

5: *Vase. Blue glass with applied loops. Loetz. Designed by Michael Powolny for J&L Lobmeyr. 1918. 9".*

Photo: Jürgen Fischer.

6: *Vase. Cream over red interior glass with red glass windings. 1920s. 6¼".*

Collection: Private.

7: *Vase. Cream over blue interior glass with blue glass windings. 1920s. 9".*

Collection: Private.

1-3: Baskets. Clear glass with colored glass applied threading. Left basket is marked: Czechoslovakia. 1930s. 7½"; 7"; 7".
Collection: Kevin P. Inman.

4: Vase. Tan glass with green spots; blue threading is hand smoothed. 1930s. 8".
Collection: Kevin P. Inman.

5: Vase. Red glass with silver threading; hand smoothed. 1930s. 14".
Collection: Joe Mattis.

6: Bowl. Amber glass with red overlay extending from bottom to top; yellow glass threading on top. 1930s. 6".
Collection: Ken Donmoyer.

7: Covered bowl. Clear glass with white glass threading. 1930s. 3¾".
Collection: Ken Donmoyer.

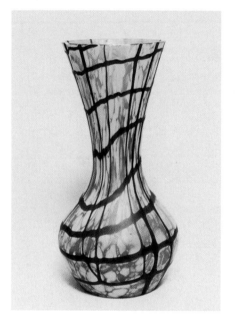

1-2
3-4
5-6 | 7-8

1: Vase. Clear glass with white spots and green windings. Blown to size after windings were applied. Marked: Czechoslovakia. 1930s. 8".
Collection: Kevin P. Inman.

2: Vase. Light brown glass with white spots and brown windings. Blown to size after windings were applied. Marked: Czechoslovakia. 1930s. 6½".
Collection: Kevin P. Inman.

3: Vase. White glass with purple-brown glass windings. Marked: Czechoslovakia. 1930s. 7¼".
Collection: Kevin P. Inman.

4: Vase. Pale green over white glass with purple-brown glass windings. Marked: Czechoslovakia. 1930s. 7½".
Collection: Kevin P. Inman.

5: Vase. Blue glass with yellow/green glass windings. Blown after windings were applied. Marked: Czechoslovakia. 1930s. 7½".
Collection: Kevin P. Inman.

6: Vase. Orange glass with purple-brown glass windings. Blown after windings were applied. Marked: Czecho-Slovakia. 1930s. 7¼".
Collection: Kevin P. Inman.

7: Vase. Clear glass with brown glass applied to base and extended to top. Marked: Czechoslovakia. 1930s. 9".
Collection: Joe Mattis.

8: Vase. Clear glass with red glass applied to base and extended to top. Marked: Czechoslovakia. 1930s. 8¼".
Collection: Joe Mattis.

$$\frac{1 - 3}{4 - 6}$$
$$7 - 9$$

All the vases have a base color glass, wound with a contrasting color; then blown in a mold to its final shape. Although all of these vases have been acquired one at a time over a period of years, it is obvious that they were made from the same two molds.

1-3:   *Vases. Kralik. 1930s. 6"; 7¾"; 6".*
Collection: Joe Mattis.

4-6:   *Vases. Kralik. Marked: Czechoslovakia. 1930s. All 6".*
Collection: Kevin P. Inman.

7-9:   *Vases. Kralik. Marked: Czechoslovakia. 1930s. All 7¾".*
Collection: Kevin P. Inman.

$$\frac{1 - 2}{3 - 5}$$
$$6 - 8$$

All have a base color glass, decorated with a contrasting color; then blown in a mold.

1-2:   *Vases. 1930s. 7".*
    Collection: Kevin P. Inman.

3:   *Covered jar. 1930s. 5".*
    Collection: Joe Mattis.

4:   *Covered bowl. Kralik. Marked: Czechoslovakia. 1930s. 7¾".*
    Collection: Joe Mattis.

5:   *Covered jar. Clear glass feet. 1930s. 5".*
    Collection: Joe Mattis.

6-8:   *Vases. Left vase is marked: Made in Czechoslovakia. Center and right vases are marked: Czechoslovakia. 1930s. 7¾"; 8¼"; 8¼".*
    Collection: Joe Mattis.

$$\frac{1-4}{5-7}$$
$$\overline{8\,|\,9\,|\,10}$$

1: Basket. Green and white with black handle. Marked: Czechoslovakia. 1930s. 9".
Collection: Kevin P. Inman.

2: Basket. Purple glass with amber prunts and handle. 1930s. 9¼".
Collection: Kevin P. Inman.

3: Basket. Yellow with black rim and handle. Marked: Czechoslovakia. 1930s. 5½".
Collection: Kevin P. Inman.

4: Basket. White glass with orange trailing; blue rim and handle. Marked: Made in Czechoslovakia. 1930s. 7".
Collection: Kevin P. Inman.

5-7: Covered jars. Feet are made in the "Italian style." 1930s. 6"; 6½"; 7".
Collection: Joe Mattis.

8: Vase. White glass with red decoration. Black rigaree handles. Marked: Czechoslovakia. 1930s. 6½".
Collection: Joe Mattis.

9: Vase. Orange glass with mottled decoration; black applied rigaree handles. 1930s. 6¼".
Collection:Kevin P. Inman.

10: Vase. Orange with brown streaking. 1930s. 11¾".
Collection: Joe Mattis.

1 - 3
4 - 7
8-10	11-13

Spatter glass is made by rolling a cylinder of hot glass over a carefully laid out design of crushed cullet. The gather is then reheated and mold blown.

1-3: Spatter glass baskets. 1930s. 6"; 6½"; 7½".

Collection: Kevin P. Inman.

4: Spatter glass vase. Marked: Czechoslovakia. 1930s. 9".

5: Spatter glass vase. Marked: Czechoslovakia. 1930s. 5¾".

6: Spatter glass vase. Marked: Made in Czechoslovakia. 1930s. 8½".

7: Spatter glass vase. 1930s. 8¾".

8: Spatter glass vase. 1930s. 9¼".

9: Spatter glass vase. Molded mark: Czecho Slovakia. 1930s. 6½".

10: Spatter glass vase. 1930s. 8¼".

11-13: Spatter glass covered jars. Applied black feet; this type of foot is often called "rocket ship" foot. Right jar has pressed in the foot: Czechoslovakia. 1930s. 7"; 7"; 6".

4-13 are from the collection of Joe Mattis.

1 - 5

6 - 8

9-10 | 11-12

1-5: *Vases. Applied "rocket ship" feet. 1930s. Sizes range from 5¾" to 8½".*
Collection: Joe Mattis.

6-8: *Covered jars. 1930s. 8"; 7¼"; 8¼".*
Collection: Joe Mattis.

9-10: *Covered jars. Left jar is marked: Czechoslovakia. 1930s. 9½"; 9¾".*
Collection: Joe Mattis.

11-12: *Vases. Blue applied "rocket ship" feet. 1930s. 8"; 6½".*
Collection: Joe Mattis.

$$\begin{array}{c|c} \multicolumn{2}{c}{1 - 4} \\ \hline \multicolumn{2}{c}{5 - 7} \\ \hline 8 & 9 - 11 \end{array}$$

1-4:   Covered dresser jars. #2 is marked in gold: Made in Czechoslovakia. #3 is marked: Czechoslovakia. 1930s. 5"; 7¾"; 5"; 3½".
Collection: Joe Mattis.

5-7:   Spatter glass candlesticks and bowl. Orange-red glass with multiple colors of glass marvered smooth. 1930s. 4¾"; 5¼".
Collection: Joe Mattis.

8:   Spatter glass vase. 1930s. 12¼".
Collection: Joe Mattis.

9-11:   Fan vases. Left is marked: Czechoslovakia. Right is marked: Made in Czechoslovakia. 1930s. 7¾"; 7¼"; 7¾".
Collection: Kevin P. Inman.

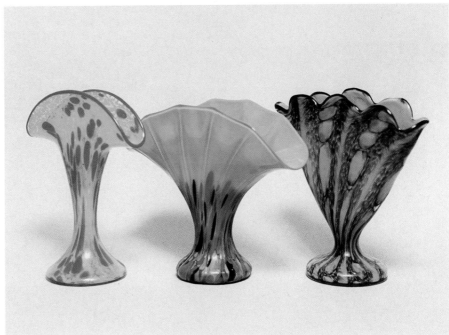

1-3: *Baskets. 1930s. 10"; 7½"; 10".*
Collection: Kevin P. Inman.

4-5: *Bowls. Hand shaped. 1930s. 5"; 5".*
Collection: Kevin P. Inman.

6-7: *Vases. Left is marked: Made in Czechoslovakia. 1930s. 12"; 6".*
Collection: Joe Mattis.

8: *Footed bowl. 1930s. 6¼".*
Collection: Ken Donmoyer.

$$\frac{1 - 4}{5}$$
6 | 7 - 8

1-4: *Opal glass, with multiple colors marvered smooth. Marked: Czechoslovakia. 1930s. 6¾"; 8"; 8"; 6".*
Collection: Kevin P. Inman.

5: *Millifiori bowl. 1930s. 13" diameter.*
Collection: Kevin P. Inman.

6: *Pitcher. Kralik. Marked: Czechoslovakia. 1930s. 8½".*
Collection: Joe Mattis.

7-8: *Millifiori vases. Black over bright orange. Left vase is marked: Czechoslovakia. 1930s. 4½"; 9½".*
Collection: Kevin P. Inman.

Thin wafers of millifiori cane are picked up on a cylinder of hot glass, reheated, then mold-blown to produce the type of glassware shown on this page.

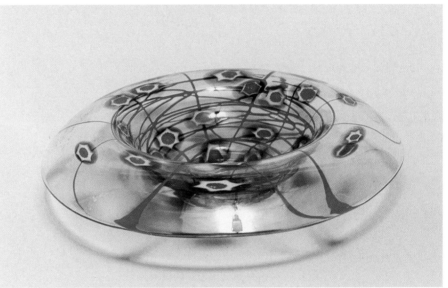

1 - 2
3 - 5
6 - 8

1-2: *Millifiori bowl and vase.*
1930s. 5½"; 6½".
Collection: Kevin P. Inman.

3 and 5: Baskets. Vaseline glass,
with multiple colors. 1930s.
7"; 9".
Collection: Kevin P. Inman.

4: *Basket. Clear with green*
handle. Marked: Made in
Czecho-Slovakia. 1930s.
6½".
Collection: Kevin P. Inman.

6: *Vase. Cream with orange*
overlay, hand smoothed.
Marked: Czechoslovakia.
1930s. 5½".
Collection: Joe Mattis.

7: *Vase. White with peach lines*
and multicolor spatter, hand
smoothed. Marked: Made in
Czechoslovakia. 1930s. 8¾".
Collection: Joe Mattis.

8: *Vase. White with blue overlay,*
hand smoothed. Marked:
Czechoslovakia. 1930s. 7¼".
Collection: Joe Mattis.

$$\frac{1 - 3}{4 - 7}$$
$$8 - 11$$

1-3:   Covered jars. Colored glass with clear overlay. Right jar has a paper label: Made in Czecho-Slovakia. 1930s. All 7".
Collection: Joe Mattis.

4-7:   Baskets. Yellow basket is marked: Czechoslovakia. Blue basket is marked: Czecho Slovakia. 1930s. 10"; 11"; 8"; 8¼".
Collection: Joe Mattis.

8:    Basket. "Tango" orange with black rim and handle. Marked: Made in Czechoslovakia. 1930s. 7".
Collection: Kevin P. Inman.

9:    Basket. Orange with black overlay; black handle. Overlay has silver flecks. Marked: Made in Czechoslovakia. 1930s. 10½".
Collection:Kevin P. Inman.

10:    Basket. Orange with clear overlay; black rim and handle. Overlay has pressed leaves and flower. 1930s. 7½".
Collection: Kevin P. Inman.

11:    Basket. "Tango" orange with clear overlay; white rim and clear handle. 1930s. 8½".
Collection: Kevin P. Inman.

1 - 2
3 - 4
5 | 6 | 7

1: Candlestick. Blue with white handles. Paper label: Czechoslovakia. 1930s. 3½".
Collection: Kevin P. Inman.

2: Vase. Blue glass with white applied rigaree. Paper label: 1886 ERPHYLA. 1930s. 7½".
Collection: Kevin P. Inman.

3-4: Vases. Colored vase with black rim. Marked: Made in Czechoslovakia. 1930s. 7".
Collection: Joe Mattis.

5: Fan vase. blue glass with white inclusions. 1930s. 12½".
Collection: Joe Mattis.

6: Vase. Yellow with blue extending from base, hand smoothed. 1930s. 10¾".
Collection: Joe Mattis.

7: Vase. Clear glass with lavender mottling; brown and yellow extending from base, hand smoothed. 1930s. 11".
Collection: Joe Mattis.

```
      1
   ─────────
      2
   ─────────
   3 │ 4 │ 5
```

1: *Glue chipped bowl. 1930s. 5½".*
Collection: Joe Mattis.

2: *Glue chipped bowl. 1930s. 3".*
Collection: Ken Donmoyer.

3: *Pitcher with lid. Amber glass, with orange overlay pulled from base to top. 1930s. 11¾".*
Collection: Joe Mattis.

4: *Pitcher. Orange glass, with brown granite glass; orange prunts and handle. 1930s. 19½".*
Collection: Joe Mattis.

5: *Glue chipped vase. Marked: Czechoslovakia. 1930s. 7¾".*
Collection: : Joe Mattis.

$$\frac{1 - 2}{3 - 5}$$
$$\overline{6 - 7}$$

1-2:   Vases. Blue glass with multicolors; blown and hand smoothed. 1930s. 8"; 10".
Collection: Joe Mattis.

3-5:   Vases. Base color glass, with decoration blown and hand smoothed. Middle vase is marked: Made in Czechoslovakia. 1930s. 5½"; 5¼"; 6¼".
Collection: Joe Mattis.

6-7:   Vase and bowl. Dark purple with paisley pattern; blown and hand smoothed.1930s. 7"; 5".
Collection: Joe Mattis.

$$\frac{\begin{array}{c} 1 - 2 \\ \hline 3 - 5 \end{array}}{6 \mid 7 - 9}$$

1-2: Candlesticks. Brownish-purple over white cased glass. 1930s. 9¾".

Collection: Joe Mattis.

...wl and candlesticks. 1930s. 7½"; 8¼".

...ction: Joe Mattis.

...White enamel mark: Czecho-Slovakia. 1930s. 11".

...on: Joe Mattis.

7-9: Vases and candlestick. Candlestick has paper label: G L Taylor, Jewelers, Optical Parlors, 991 Bloor St. West, Toronto. Right vase is marked: Czechoslovakia. 1930s. 8"; 10½"; 10¾".

Collection: Joe Mattis.

1: *Deco lamp. Multi-colored glass shade.
   Metal base has been repainted. 1930s. 9˝.*
   Collection: Joe Mattis.

2: *Lamp. Multi-colored glass beads and
   flowers. 1930s. 5½"*
   Collection: Charles and Barbara Plummer.

3: *Deco lamp. Multi-colored glass shade.
   Metal base has been repainted. 1930s.
   11".*
   Collection: Joe Mattis.

4: *Deco lamp. Multi-colored glass shade.
   Original paint on base. 1930s. 22".*
   Collection: Ken Donmoyer.

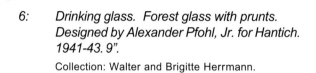

6:   *Drinking glass. Forest glass with prunts.*
Designed by Alexander Pfohl, Jr. for Hantich.
1941-43. 9".

Collection: Walter and Brigitte Herrmann.

1-3: Console bowl and candlesticks. Red and black cased glass. Candlesticks are marked: Czechoslovakia. 1930s. 6"; 8¾".
Collection: Joe Mattis.

4-6: Console bowl and candlesticks. Orange and black cased glass. Candlesticks are marked: Czechoslovakia. 1930s. 3½"; bowl is 11" diameter.
Collection: Joe Mattis.

7-9: Glasses. Marked: Made in Czecho-Slovakia. 1930s. 2¾".
Collection: Joe Mattis.

10-11: Three-handled Tango vases. Both have clear casing. Left vase has blue rim and handles. Right vase has black rim and handles. 1930s. 5"; 4½".
Collection: Joe Mattis.

$$\frac{1}{\frac{2\text{-}3}{4\mid 5}}$$

1: *Two-handled tazza. 1930s. 3¾".*
Collection: Joe Mattis.

2-3: *Tango vases. Green vase has paper label: Made in Czechoslovakia. 1930s. 6½".*
Collection: Joe Mattis.

4: *Bird decanter. Palda. Mid-1930s. 10".*
Collection: Elaine Palda Swiler.

5: *Duck decanter. Palda. Mid-1930s. 11".*
Collection: Charles and Barbara Plummer.

1	2-3
4	- 7
8	9

1:    *Tango vase. Brilliant red with black trim. 1930s. 8".*
Collection: Joe Mattis.

2-3:   *Vases. Orange and clear cased glass, with black trim. 1930s. 7¼"; 10¾".*
Collection: Joe Mattis.

4-7:   *Vases. Orange glass with various black and brown decorations. Tallest vase is marked: Czecho Slovakia. 1930s. 7"; 8½"; 5"; 7¼".*
Collection: Joe Mattis.

8:    *Covered bowl. Marked: Czecho-Slovakia. 1930s. 5¾".*
Collection: Joe Mattis.

9:    *Three-handled vase. Loetz. Marked: Czecho-Slovakia. 1930s. 5".*
Collection: Joe Mattis.

$$\begin{array}{c|c} 1 & 2 \\ \hline 3 & - & 4 \\ \hline 5 & 6 \end{array}$$

1: *Vase. Amber with pulled blue design. Loetz. 1930s. 12".*
Collection: Glass Museum Nový Bor.

2: *Vase. Decorated in the Venetian manner. Loetz. 1930s. 11".*
Collection: Glass Museum Nový Bor.

3-4: *Vase and covered bowl. Blue Phänomen decoration. Loetz. Bowl is marked: Czecho-Slovakia. 1930s. 8¼"; 6½".*
Collection: Joe Mattis.

5: *Vase with metal cage. Cased clear, over colors, over white. Kralik. Marked: Czechoslovakia. 1930s. 8¾".*
Collection: Joe Mattis.

6: *Vase in metal cage. Kralik. Marked: Czechoslovakia. 1930s. 6¾".*
Collection: Joe Mattis.

$$\frac{1}{\frac{2}{3\,|\,4}}$$

1: *Vase. Yellow and blue Phänomen. Loetz. Variation of product #1146. 1925-30. 7".*
Collection: Private.

2: *Bowl. Orange and black cased with black ball feet. Marked: Czechoslovakia. 1930s. 7¼.*
Collection: Joe Mattis.

3: *Vase. Cobalt Phänomen. Loetz. 1930s. 4¾".*
Collection: Private.

4: *Tango vase. Loetz. Marked: Czecho-Slovakia. 1930s. 5¾".*
Collection: Private.

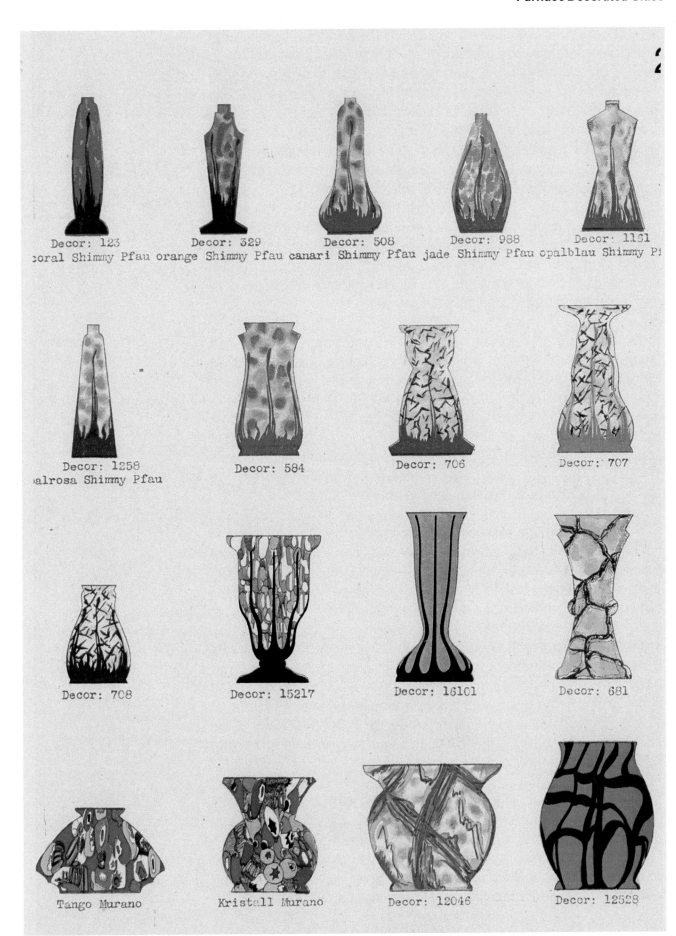

Decor: 123
coral Shimmy Pfau

Decor: 329
orange Shimmy Pfau

Decor: 508
canari Shimmy Pfau

Decor: 988
jade Shimmy Pfau

Decor: 1161
opalblau Shimmy Pf

Decor: 1258
alrosa Shimmy Pfau

Decor: 584

Decor: 706

Decor: 707

Decor: 708

Decor: 15217

Decor: 16101

Decor: 681

Tango Murano

Kristall Murano

Decor: 12046

Decor: 12528

Rückl catalog used around 1931. Spatterware produced by Rückl was designated either by a number or a catchy name. Some of the names are shown in the catalog page; others were: Pierrot, Marmor, and Metallit.

Despite its well-earned reputation for handmade glass, the Czech glass industry also produced an impressive amount of pressed glass. Typically the production of pressed glass can be directly connected to the world economy. During the early years of the Czech Republic (1920-23), pressed glass exports accounted for only 39 million Crowns as compared to 317 million Crowns for hollow glass (average per year). This translates to 5,000 barrels vs. 66,000 barrels. By 1935, hollow glass exports had fallen to 39,000 barrels (down 41%) and pressed glass exports rose to 12,500 barrels (up 250%).

A great deal of the pressed glass consisted of inexpensive dresser sets, tableware, perfume bottles and stoppers. The Carr-Lowrey Company in Baltimore, MD, was reported to import 72,000 stoppers a week prior to World War I. After World War I, sales of pressed glass increased in every category.

As shown in the table on page 3, Great Britain and the USA became the destination for most of the Czech glass during the 1920s and 1930s. Some of the glass was impressed with the word Czechoslovakia, but a great deal was marked only with a paper label. Quite often the importer/retailer would supply the factory with labels that may or may not have included the country of origin. The Barolac label sometimes mentions Czechoslovakia and sometimes it doesn't. Barolac was the name used by the English merchant John Jenkins on pressed glass made in Czechoslovakia between the wars.

The production of pressed glass centered around the area of Jablonec. The Riedel glassworks in Polubný was especially popular with the independent entrepreneurs Heinrich Hoffmann and Henry Gunther Schlevogt. Schlevogt worked for Hoffmann from 1927 to 1930 and had married Hoffmann's daughter Charlotte. Both Heinrich Hoffmann and Henry Schlevogt were second generation glass men. Hoffmann's father, Franz, began making jewelry and door/drawer knobs in 1867 in the Jablonec area; Heinrich took over in 1900. Schlevogt's father, Curt, also from Jablonec, specialized in glass jewelry and bead work. Heinrich and Henry remained life-long friends and associates. When Schlevogt left the Hoffmann firm he took with him many of the projects he had been working on and several molds that he and Hoffmann had developed.

It was a common practice for Hoffmann to include his butterfly trademark in his molds and undoubtedly some of the molds Schlevogt took with him included the trademark. The close friendship between the two led to a co-mingling of designs and products which has caused some problems for collectors of their glass. Most historians, however, feel that positive attribution between the firms is usually irrelevant.

In 1934, at the Leipzig spring fair, Schlevogt unveiled his newly developed "Ingrid" line, a large variety of dresser items, accessories, and vases intended to rival the French firm Lalique's molded glass.

Both Hoffmann and Schlevogt availed themselves of the services of the best designers in the glass industry. They also employed designers full time to create particular motifs. František Pazourek, one of Professor Drahoňovský's most talented and famous pupils, designed countless perfume stoppers based upon Drahoňovský's glyptics. Pazourek worked for Hoffmann from 1929 until 1931 and continued to contribute occasional designs up to 1939. In 1937, Schlevogt won a Grand Prize in Paris for a nude sculpture designed by Ena Rottenberg.

The very nature of pressed glass makes it difficult to date or attribute to a specific factory. Knowing what colors were produced at various times is helpful and the amount of post-production hand-finishing can be an indication of age.

We were able to locate only a small amount of pressed glass to photograph, since we required each piece to be positively marked, either impressed in the glass or with an original label. We often see pressed glass that we are absolutely sure is from Bohemia but without a definitive mark or label.

Pin tray. Hoffmann. Pressed butterfly mark. 1930s. 2½" wide.
Collection: Private.

Pin tray. Hoffmann. Pressed butterfly mark. 1930s. 2¾" wide.
Collection: Private.

1: *"Ingrid" candleholder. Schlevogt. 1934-45. 7½".*
Collection: Private.

2: *Pin trays in filigree holder. 1930s. 8".*
Collection: Ken Donmoyer.

3: *Decanter and glasses. 1920s and '30s. 10" & 2¼".*
Collection: Ken Donmoyer.

4: *Dresser boxes. 1930s. Far right box is 2½" high.*
Collection: Charles and Barbara Plummer.

1: Vase. Raised bird pattern, with solid brass handles
    and filigree.   Molded mark: Czechoslovakia.
    1920s-30s. 11".
    Collection: Private.

2: Salt and pepper shakers. All marked:
    Czechoslovakia. Average 2" high.
    Collection: Charles and Barbara Plummer.

3: Vase. Raised cherries. Molded mark:
    Czechoslovakia. 1920s-30s. 7".
    Collection: Private.

4: Perfume, hair receiver, atomizer, and flower-
    shaped salt and pepper shakers with glass tops.
    All marked: Czechoslovakia. 1920s-30s. Average
    3" high.
    Collection: Charles and Barbara Plummer.

5: Vase. Raised horses. Molded mark:
    Czechoslovakia. 1920s-30s. 6½".
    Collection: Private.

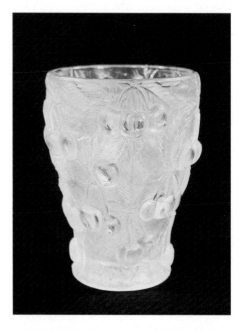

Some of the first objects to be made of glass in Egypt and Rome were figurines and not a century has passed without someone, somewhere producing some form of these stylized, little icons. After all these centuries and the rapid growth of worldwide glass making, you would think that nothing new could have been created as late as the 20th year of the 20th century. Never-the-less, events had been set in motion that redefined empires and industries. When Bohemia became part of the newly formed Republic of Czechoslovakia, there was an opportunity for the Czech culture to emerge as an economic force.

With the creation of the Železný Brod Glass School in 1920, the new Republic secured an opportunity for Czech speaking students and faculty to enter the higher echelons of the glass industry. One of the first professors at Železný Brod was Jaroslav Brychta, a trained sculptor and a graduate of Drahoňovský's and Kafka's modeling school. Upon graduation from the Academy of Applied Art in Prague, Brychta aspired to a career as a sculptor and was well on his way when he was persuaded to accept a professorship at the Glass School.

Circumstances again were at work at the Glass School. Brychta's unique mind and a wholly inadequate budget forced him to set aside plans for sculpting and engraving, and to turn to something more practical. Železný Brod is located just south of Jablonec, an area long famous for its bead production and home to many small shops doing custom work. Since the Železný Brod Glass School taught bead making, it didn't take long for the art of Brychta to join with the craft of bead making.

Their first efforts produced pins, hatpins, and other simple jewelry, fashioned by threading specially designed beads and lamp worked rods on string or wire. The school proudly exhibited these pieces at their first anniversary exposition in 1921. For the next three years, Brychta expanded his designs to include figurines (made of beads and rods) of people engaged in sports and other activities that appealed to the Czech people. Hikers, boxers, and football players were just a few of the many designs created in the early years of the process. When the Art Deco exhibit closed in Paris in 1925, the school had garnered a Grand Prize and Brychta won gold and silver medals.

The exceptional showing in Paris guaranteed the future of the figurine production. Characters from Czech mythology, opera, fairy tales, and song inspired Brychta and his students to create even more fanciful figures. Until 1925, all the figurines were produced by either (or a combination) of two methods: stringing pre-formed beads on a wire or manipulating solid glass rods over a gas flame.

FIGURINES

Additional experimentation and the development of new gas technologies, allowed the creation of the fantastic creatures for which Brychta is famous. The new modeling technique resulted in the production of figures made from a single rod, with legs, antlers, and other extensions pulled from (or attached to) the main part of the body. By 1926, the school was experimenting with lamp work that involved blowing hollow figurines from softened rods. The objects were minutely detailed, using tweezers and miniature tools created especially for the lamp workers.

At this point, the lamp work produced at Železný Brod rivaled the products of the lamp workers in Lauscha, Thüringen, and Vienna (most notably, the Bimini Werkstätte). Although all lamp workers produced similar work, the mind of Brychta was clearly seen in the figurines from Železný Brod.

Brychta and his students never stopped experimenting. They combined various techniques to produce complicated designs for the local glass works, that were well staffed with the school's graduates. Other, independent designers also contributed numerous designs for the glass producers in the area.

In 1928, Brychta arranged for his students to work with the glass blowers at the Harrach glassworks in Nový Svět. There they explored the many ramifications of making large, multi-colored figurines of people. Brychta learned a great deal about the mechanics of hot glass working at Nový Svět and on a visit to Murano where the process had been carried on for many years. When the school built its own small furnace in 1934, Brychta had the chance to put together a successful team of glass chemists and blowers and move forward with his designs.

In the mid-1930s, Brychta produced his first figurines made from molten glass by a team of glass makers. The process of working with hot glass at the furnace provided the designers the opportunity to create figurines that could be easily "clothed" in recognizable costumes, such as sailors, ball players, doctors, firemen, and such.

Professor Brychta spent 40 years at Železný Brod (the school was closed from 1948-1952) and created unknown thousands of designs. The production began in 1920 and was not interrupted even during World War II. Since 1945, hundreds of designers have provided countless models for the numerous large and small glass works. Each decade has brought forth the humorous, romantic, and patriotic characters of the Czech people as depicted by the figurines. Several glass houses have tried to duplicate the figurines, but rarely achieve the results of the Železný Brod glass producers.

Defining the Various Types of Figurines

The vast majority of figurines available to collectors are made by one of two processes: made from a solid rod by a single lamp worker, or made from molten glass by a team of glass workers. Recognizing the various techniques can help in dating and appreciating the difficulty in the development of the figurines.

As is often the case, the Czech word for each technique has no exact equivalent in English. We arrived at the following terms and descriptions after careful consultation with several authorities on the subject.

◆ Drátkové (wired or stitched) – specially formed beads are strung together on wire to create the figures. The oldest technique, although string was also used in the first year of production. (See picture # 2 on page 83.)

◆ Foukané (blown) – figurines blown from a solid rod by a lamp worker. (See picture #1 on page 83.)

◆ Hutní (glass hut) – solid glass figurines made from molten glass by a team of glass workers. (See picture #3 on page 84.)

◆ Modelované (modeled) – solid rods worked at the lamp by pulling, stretching, flattening, etc. It differs from Tažené as it is more complex and involves shaping the glass in unusual ways. (See picture #6 on page 84.)

◆ Natrhávané (no English) – the figure is first constructed using the Modelované or Tažené technique, then it is finished by touching elements of the design with a hot glass rod that leaves a pattern of raised glass on the surface. (See pictures #3-4 on page 83.)

◆ Tažené (drawn) – one of the earliest techniques. A lamp worker manipulates a softened glass rod to produce a simple figurine. Some times additional bits of hot glass were applied to form features or extremities. (See pictures # 5-7 on page 83.)

Bird pin. Stitched technique.
Possibly designed by Brychta.
1920s. 1½" long.
Museum of Glass and Jewelry, Jablonec.

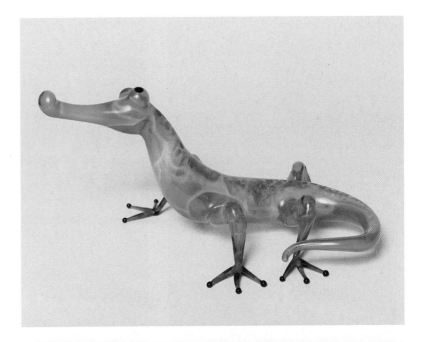

	1	
	2	
3-4		5-7

1:   Crocodile. Blown technique. Designed by Miloslav Janků in the 1940s. 9" long. Signed: M. Janků.

2:   Handball players. Wired technique. Designed by Jaroslav Brychta in 1920s. Figures are 5½" high.

3-4:   Female figurines. Glass rods, using the Natrhavané technique. 1920s. 3½"; 5¼".

5-7:   Male figurines. Glass rods, using the drawn technique. 1940s. 3½"; 4"; 3½".

All from the collection of the Museum of Glass and Jewelry, Jablonec.

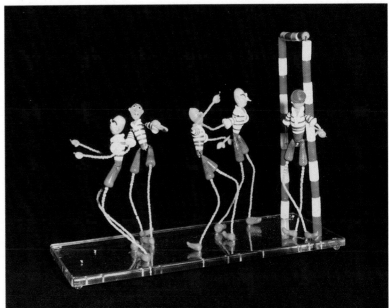

1 2
3 4
5 6

1: *Male figurine. Stitched technique. Designed by Jaroslav Brychta in 1920s. 4".*
Collection: Irma and Richard Hosch.

2: *Male figurine. Stitched technique. Designed by Jaroslav Brychta in 1920s. 5".*

3: *Woman with ducks. Glass house technique. Designed by Železný Brod School. 1930s. 5¼".*

4: *Man with banner. Glass House technique. Designed by Železný Brod School. 1930s. 5¼".*

5: *Chickens pulling man on cart. Drawn technique. 1940s. 2¾".*

6: *Octopus in seaweed. Part of a set called Water World. Designed by Jaroslav Brychta in the 1920s. Modeled technique. 6".*

Nos. 2-6 are from the collection of the Museum of Glass and Jewelry in Jablonec.

$$\frac{\dfrac{1}{2}}{3 \mid 4 \mid 5}$$

1: *Flower. Separate pieces of glass, fused together. Designed by Železný Brod Glass School. 1920s. 2½" wide.*

Collection: Museum of Glass and Jewelry, Jablonec.

2: *Man riding pig. Blown pig; Man is drawn technique; Man's head is Natrhavané technique. 1930s. 3¼".*

Collection: Museum of Glass and Jewelry, Jablonec.

3: *Child figurine. Glass house technique. Designed and executed by Ateliery Bor. 1950s. 3½".*

Collection: Glass Museum Nový Bor.

4: *Young girl with a bag. Glass house technique. Designed and executed by Ateliery Bor. 1950s. 6".*

Collection: Glass Museum Nový Bor.

5: *Clown. Glass house technique. 1930s. 6½".*

Collection: Private.

Painting a design or decoration on glass is one of the oldest methods of refining. By the second century AD (possibly even before) painters were applying their art to glass vessels. Like cutting and engraving, however, these skills were mostly abandoned until the 15th century.

By 1915, there was very little left to be discovered concerning the technology of painting on glass. Mastering the technical aspects of the materials involved left the artists free to experiment with new applications and techniques. The Glass Schools played an important role by encouraging their students to venture into previously untried ways of using common materials.

The transparent enamel, so beautifully used by Kothgasser and Mohn a century earlier, took on a whole new appearance when applied as a geometric flower. Red and yellow stains, previously used to simulate cased glass, were applied as part of the decoration. Thickly applied opaque enamels made single thickness glass appear as overlay that had been cut.

Of all the refining processes, none is so technically diverse as the application of stains and enamels. Mastering the endless combinations of variables would take several lifetimes. Working in such a field forced each painter to specialize in techniques that could be mastered profitably; firms employing ten or more painters would try to have at least one specialist for each technique.

Anyone aspiring to become a painter would typically enter one of the glass technical schools (Nový Bor, Kamenický Šenov, or Železný Brod) at age 14. During vacation breaks, students usually worked for a local painter. After graduation at age 17 or 18, the student could work as a journeyman in a shop or continue his education at the university level in Prague or Vienna. If he attended a university, he would receive training in modeling, sculpture, art history, and graphics. After graduation and the completion of a "masterpiece" the student would obtain a masters license allowing him to open his own shop or to teach.

Although some glass manufacturers (such as Moser, Loetz, and Harrach) employed their own artists, the execution of the painted designs was by far the provenance of the independent refiners and exporters.

Geography also influenced the designs produced. The painters working in the southern area of Bohemia developed a style and techniques different from that of their cousins working in the northeast. The town of Okrouhlá, near Nový Bor, was particularly well known for its workers specializing in gold painting and gold leaf

PAINTED AND STAINED GLASS

work. 80% to 90% of the high enamel painting, as well as the white enamel decoration we call "Mary Gregory," was produced in an area of less than 100 square miles around Nový Bor. The close proximity of the Glass Schools allowed the refiners in the north to keep up with the latest fashions, as well as to continue their traditional motifs.

This is good news for the collector and historian, for it helps, in varying degrees, to identify the *most probable* source of a particular piece of painted glassware. Often the individual peculiarities of a kiln determined the type of decoration that could be produced in a particular shop. The majority of the painters worked in a studio in their home — sometimes alone and in some cases with another family member. These home studios typically had a small kiln fueled with wood or coal. Fusing the enamel to the article required exact temperatures and timing; thus many applications were beyond the small home kiln. Despite the advanced technology available, a fairly large amount of glassware was painted with oil paint and sold in the unfired state.

From 1915 to 1945, just about every technique ever used was still in service. That included everything from drawing with a quill pen, to silk screening, and spray painting. Prior to graduation from one of the glass technical schools, each student would be thoroughly drilled in both the historical uses of stains and enamels and the most modern application of each.

The best known use of stains on glass has been in the production of what has long been known as Egermann glass. Bowls, vases, decanters and glasses, stained red or yellow, are then engraved on a stone wheel, typically with hunting or forest scenes.

Although stains can easily be mistaken for transparent enamels, the process is quite different. Enamel is basically glass, ground into a fine powder and mixed with a fluxing agent and pigment. It can be applied in numerous ways and, when fired in a kiln, it fuses to the surface of the article.

Stains, on the other hand, are chemical compounds that are almost always brushed on the glass and require a long and carefully controlled firing process. Red stain is the most difficult to produce, requiring up to five separate firings – each in a different atmosphere. Various chemical companies produced red stains that allowed for some short cuts, but for the deepest color and greatest permanence, the process was very exacting.

Modern refineries use electric kilns which can be controlled to plus or minus one degree and are piped to allow exactly the desired gas mixture to be injected into the kiln. In the 1920s and '30s, it was common practice for the kiln operator to place various objects in the kiln to produce the required atmosphere. A lump of smoldering coal produced carbon monoxide and sulfur dioxide, both necessary in the production of red stain. At least one of the five separate firings in the kiln was at a greatly reduced oxygen content. Due to the many variables involved, especially in the glass formulas, numerous pieces would emerge with a glowing iridescence (like gasoline on water) and are prized today more than the more perfect pieces.

Throughout the Art Deco period the same red and yellow stains, along with black, were used in a variety of motifs. Rather than a background for engraved scenes, the stains were applied in a distinct pattern and were often used in conjunction with geometric cutting.

The Art Deco period was especially renowned for experimenting with combinations of refining techniques. Stains combined with enamel, ...with engraving, ...with cutting, or all combined, appear on Deco glassware.

The Glass Schools were especially adept at the creation of modern designs in every discipline, and most contemporary Czech historians can distinguish between the glass designed at the Nový Bor Glass School and that designed at the school in Kamenický Šenov.

Certain professors at each school were responsible for a large number of documented designs and their influence is often obvious to today's collectors. One particularly good example of this is the complicated black line paintings designed by Adolf Beckert (Kamenický Šenov) for Friedrich Pietsch and others (see page 100). Beckert and his students also designed numerous black silhouettes inspired by the German artist Karl Wilhelm Diefenbach.

The transition from Art Nouveau to Art Deco motifs was more complicated than it might seem. For the most part, Art Nouveau painting was rather straightforward in its technique. Deco motifs often combined enameling with cutting, staining, sand-blasting, and a variety of application techniques that were being developed specifically for a particular design.

The process of applying colored stains on glass has not changed much since it was first developed by Friedrich Egermann early in the 19th century. Despite the advancements in technology and chemical formulas, the methodology used in the 1920s and '30s remained basically the same. During this time period just about every refinery had the capability for staining glass, whether they used it or not.

In addition to the original colors of yellow and red (including cranberry), black stain was also often used in the Deco period. The extensive use of transparent enamels and the specialized techniques developed for applying them often cause the modern day collector to wonder just how a colored decoration was executed.

During the 1920s and '30s one of the most prolific producers of red or yellow stained glass was the Karl Goldberg refineries. Goldberg named his Egermann line after the famous painter and included a postage stamp size label with Egermann's picture on each piece.

At the end of World War I, tourists returned to Prague and the spa areas and usually went home with one or more items featuring hunt scenes or castles with Rococo strap work. To this day, Czech refineries are producing Egermann-type glass based upon the original formulas and motifs.

The inventions involving sandblasting and spray painting played nicely into the hands of the refiners. Air brush work was ideal for applying free-hand designs and a great variety of motifs using standard masking techniques. The faculty and the students at the Glass Schools were hard pressed to provide enough new motifs for the painters eager to supply the newest fashions.

Students at the three Glass Schools must have felt a little sense of history as they went from a class on air brushing to a class on painting with a feather.

Feather painting was popular in the Art Deco period and remains a well used technology even today. Federzeichnung -- pen sketching or pen and ink drawing -- was used extensively by the J.M. Pohl workshop in Nový Bor. Many of Pohl's best decorations involved quill pen drawings: "The Hay Harvest," "Stagecoach," and "The Shepherds." Copies of these can be seen on page 113.

Another technique using the quill pen is Federdecor -- using a feather pen to create the fine squiggly lines (typically of silver or gold), such as between the panels on Lištované glass. Modern day painters use regular nib drawing pens for their pen sketches, but occasionally revert to the quill pen for special work.

The photographs in this section show the wide variety of painting techniques used by Bohemian refiners.

1	2	
3	4	
5	6	7

1: *Vase. Designed at the Kamenický Šenov Glass School. Paper label: St.St. 1920s. 4½".*
Collection: Glass Museum Kamenický Šenov.

2: *Vase. Oertel. 1935-55. 7½".*
Collection: Glass Museum Nový Bor.

3: *Vase. Designed at the Kamenický Šenov Glass School. Paper label: St.St. 1925. 8½".*
Collection: Glass Museum Kamenický Šenov.

4: *Beaker. Designed for the Wiener Werkstätte by Lotte Calm. Motif consists of 3 identical heads painted in black enamel. Bottom is air brushed. ≈1918. 7¼".*
Collection: Bernd Lienemann.

5-7: *3 views of a vase. Red and yellow stains. Designed at the Nový Bor Glass School. Decorated by Oertel. Similar glass was also decorated by Fritz Jenak, a student of Alexander Pfohl Jr. 1935-45. 10¼".*
Collection: Glass Museum Nový Bor.

1	2
3	4
5	6

1: *Vase. Brown bubble glass. ≈1935. 10¼".*
Collection: Glass Museum Nový Bor.

2: *Vase. Jílek Brothers. ≈1935. 6".*
Collection: Glass Museum Nový Bor.

3: *Vase. Designed at the Nový Bor Glass School. 1924. 7½".*
Collection: Glass Museum Nový Bor.

4: *Vase. Jílek Brothers; refined in Nový Bor. 1935. 9½".*
Collection: Glass Museum Nový Bor.

5: *Covered Pokal. St. Michael and Satan. Designed at the Nový Bor Glass School. ≈1930s. 16¾".*
Collection: Glass Museum Nový Bor.

6: *Vase. Karl Goldberg. ≈1930. 8".*
Collection: Glass Museum Nový Bor.

1: *Covered jar. 1915-25. 10½".*
Collection: Glass Museum Nový Bor.

2: *Vase. 1915-25. 8½".*
Collection: Glass Museum Nový Bor.

3: *Covered jar. Oertel. 1930s. 11½".*
Collection: Oertel Museum.

4: *Vase. Designed at the Kamenický Šenov Glass School. Marked: M (in a circle); K.K.F-S.ST.; W.R. ≈1915. 9½".*
Collection: Glass Museum Kamenický Šenov.

5: *Vase. Designed at the Kamenický Šenov Glass School. Marked: M (in a circle); K.K.F-S.ST.; T.A. ≈1918. 12½".*
Collection: Glass Museum Kamenický Šenov.

6: *Vase. Designed at the Nový Bor Glass School. Marked: HFS. 1915-25. 9".*
Collection: Glass Museum Nový Bor.

7: *Decanter. Designed at the Kamenický Šenov Glass School. 1910-20. 9½".*
Collection: Glass Museum Kamenický Šenov.

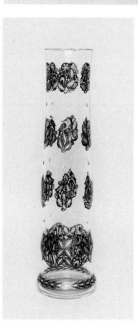

1	2
3 - 4	
5	6	7

1: Vase. Designed at the Kamenický Šenov Glass School. Marked: K.K.F-S. ST. Paper label: St.St. 1910-15. 10½".
Collection: Glass Museum Kamenický Šenov.

2: Vase. Designed at the Kamenický Šenov Glass School. 1920s-30s. 5¼".
Collection: Glass Museum Kamenický Šenov.

3: Vase. 1935-1960. 6½".
Collection: Glass Museum Nový Bor.

4: Vase. 1930s. 6".
Collection: Glass Museum Nový Bor.

Numerous refineries in Nový Bor used the motif shown on Nos. 3 and 4.

5: Vase. Designed at the Kamenický Šenov Glass School. Paper label: St.St. 1915-25. 7".
Collection: Glass Museum Kamenický Šenov.

6: Vase. Designed at the Kamenický Šenov Glass School. Paper label: St.St. 1920s. 4¾".
Collection: Glass Museum Kamenický Šenov.

7: Vase. Designed at the Kamenický Šenov Glass School. 1920s. 6¼".
Collection: Glass Museum Kamenický Šenov.

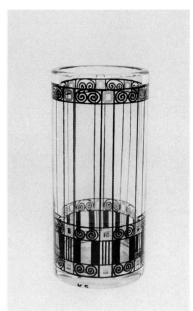

All the items on this page were designed and painted by Alexander Pfohl, Jr. for members of his family.

1:    *Vase. 1943. 8½".*

2:    *Vase. 1939. 8".*

3-4:   *Two views of a vase. "Noah's Ark." 1945-46. 12½".*

5-7:   *Glasses. Red stain is carefully applied to the glass. After firing, a diamond scribe is used to "scratch" the design. 1936-40. 5"; 6½"; 7¼".*

All from the collection of Walter and Brigitte Herrmann.

1	2
3	4
5	6

1: Vase. Designed by and probably executed at the Nový Bor Glass School. 1920s. 8½".
Collection: Private.

2: Vase. Designed at the Kamenický Šenov Glass School. Etched; cut; spray painted with semi-transparent enamels. 1930s. 10½".
Collection: Glass Museum Kamenický Šenov.

3-4: Two views of a vase. Designed and painted by Erwin Pfohl as his Masterpiece. The design shows his ancestors and the motto of glass painters. 1938. 13½".
Collection: Walter and Brigitte Herrmann.

5: Vase. Designed by Bruno Ried, Nový Bor. Acid etched; painted with semi-transparent enamels. ≈1925. 13¼".
Photo: Jürgen Fischer.

6: Vase. Designed by Bruno Ried, Kamenický Šenov. ≈1935. 10¼".
Photo: Jürgen Fischer.

$$\frac{1 \ | \ 2}{\frac{3 \ - \ 5}{6 \ | \ 7 \ | \ 8}}$$

1200-1500

All pieces on this page were designed at the Kamenický Šenov Glass School. See the pages on marks, especially page 125.

1: Vase. 1920s. 9½".

2: Vase. Paper label: St.St. ≈1920s. 9½".

3: Vase. 1920s. 8¼".

4: Vase. Paper label: St.St. 1920s. 8¼".

5: Vase. Marked: K.K.F-S.ST.; P.T. ≈1915. 7½".

6: Vase. Designed by Adolf Dorn. Marked: AD; K.K.F-S.St. ≈1918. 7¾".

7: Vase. Marked: F.-S.-ST. ≈1920. 7¾".

8: Vase. Paper label: St.St. 1920s. 4½".

All are in the collection of the Glass Museum Kamenický Šenov.

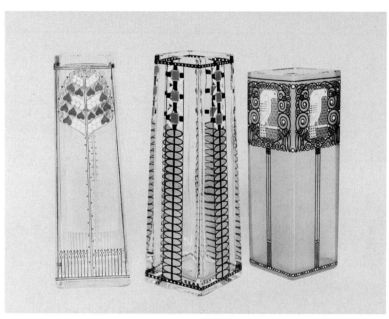

	1	2
	3	4
5	6	7

*1: Vase. Designed by Alexander Pfohl,
Jr. for Josephinenhütte. 1920. 3".*
Collection: Walter and Brigitte Herrmann.

*2: Vase. Executed by Adolf Rasche.
Marked: AR Haida. 1920-30. 4¼".*
Collection: Bernd Lienemann.

3: Covered jar. ≈1925. 4¾".
Collection: Bernd Lienemann.

*4: Vase. Designed by Alexander Pfohl,
Jr. for Josephinenhütte. Lid is
missing. ≈1921. 4¾".*
Collection: Bernd Lienemann.

*5: Vase. Black amethyst glass. An
updated Harrach design from the
mid-1800s. Marked: CZECHO
SLOVAKIA. 1930s. 8".*
Collection: Ken Donmoyer.

6: Vase. 1930s. 8½".
Collection: Ken Donmoyer.

*7: Vase. Paper label: K&M.L 4532/6,
Paar cet Paar. 1920s. 3".*
Collection: Bernd Lienemann.

1: *Vase. Designed at the Kamenický Šenov Glass School. 1920s. 5".*

Collection: Glass Museum Kamenický Šenov.

2: *Vase. ≈1925. 4¾".*

Collection: Bernd Lienemann.

3: *Bowl. Spray painted. Designed by Adolf Dorn at the Kamenický Šenov Glass School. 1930. 3¾".*

Collection: Bernd Lienemann.

4: *Vase. Designed at the Kamenický Šenov Glass School. Engraved: K.K.F-S.St. Marked in gold: T.A.; M. Paper label: St.St. ≈1910-20. 7".*

Collection: Glass Museum Kamenický Šenov.

5: *Vase. Decorated with transparent and semi-transparent enamels. 1920-25. 7¼".*

Collection: Bernd Lienemann.

6: *Vase. Designed by Josef Hoffmann for the Wiener Werkstätte. 1925. 5½".*

Collection: Bernd Lienemann.

1 | 2

3

4

1: *Goblet. Wiener Werkstätte. Marked: WW. ≈1920. 4".*
Collection: Bernd Lienemann.

2: *Goblet. Designed by Maria Vera Brunner or Josef Hoffmann for the Wiener Werkstätte. ≈1917. 7¼".*
Collection: Bernd Lienemann.

3: *Footed bowl. ≈1925. 2½".*
Collection: Bernd Lienemann.

4: *Vase. Designed by Dagobert Peche for the Wiener Werkstätte. Marked: P (with an asterisk). 1918. 6½".*
Collection: Bernd Lienemann.

2000 -2500

Karl Massanetz was one of the first painters to use the fine filigree designs which became very popular in the 1920s. Most of Massanetz's work was sold by J&L Lobmeyr in Vienna. Massanetz was killed during World War I, in 1918.

1
2
3 - 5

1: *Vase. Karl Massanetz. 1912-14. 6½".*
Collection: Bernd Lienemann.

2: *Footed bowl. Designed by Adolf Beckert at the Kamenický Šenov Glass School. Painted by Friedrich Pietsch. After 1916. 5¼".*
Collection: Private.

3: *Bowl. Designed at the Kamenický Šenov Glass School. ≈1920. 6".*
Photo: Jürgen Fischer.

4: *Bowl. Designed by Adolf Beckert. Executed by Conrath & Liebsch. ≈1915. 6".*
Photo: Jürgen Fischer.

5: *Bowl. Designed by Adolf Beckert. Executed by Friedrich Pietsch. ≈1915. 3½".*
Photo: Jürgen Fischer.

1500 -2000

Adolf Beckert designed numerous motifs for Friedrich Pietsch. Pietsch became the primary producer of "feather painting" after the death of Massanetz.

1	2
3	4
5	6

1: *Bowl. Designed at the Kamenický Šenov Glass School. 1915-20. 2¾".*
Collection: Private.

2: *Footed bowl. Designed at the Kamenický Šenov Glass School. 1915-20. 8½".*
Photo: Jürgen Fischer.

3: *Footed bowl. Motif depicts fairy tale characters. Probably executed by Friedrich Pietsch. 1915-20. 5".*
Collection: Bernd Lienemann.

4: *Footed bowl. Decorated with fairy tale characters: Little Red Riding Hood, Cinderella, Hansel and Gretel, and the little shoemaker. 1915-20. 4".*
Collection: Private.

5: *Covered jar. Designed by Adolf Beckert. Executed by Friedrich Pietsch. 1915-20. 5¾".*
Collection: Bernd Lienemann.

6: *Covered jar. Designed by Adolf Beckert for Friedrich Pietsch. After 1915. 6¾".*
Photo: Jürgen Fischer.

Karl Wilhelm Diefenbach was a trained artist and social reformer. He was born in Hadamar, Germany on February 21, 1851 and died in Capri, Italy on December 13, 1913. During his lifetime he wrote and illustrated children's books and popularized the "silhouette manner" of art work, which reached its peak between 1910 and 1920.

This illustration is from one panel of the frieze "Per Aspera ad Astra" which is on display in the Diefenbach Museum in Hadamar.

Photo: Diefenbach Museum, Hadamar, Germany.

1
___
2
___
3 | 4

1: *Bowl. Designed by Karl Pohl for the Nový Bor Glass School. Marked: Pohl. ≈1922. 3".*

Collection: Bernd Lienemann.

2: *Bowl. Black and colored opaque and transparent enamels. Designed at the Nový Bor Glass School. After 1915. 4½".*

Collection: Private.

3: *Bowl. Yellow stain; black and colored enamels. Designed at the Nový Bor Glass School. 1915-20. 3¾".*

Collection: Bernd Lienemann.

4: *Vase. Opaque enamels; red and yellow stain. Designed by Karl Pohl at the Nový Bor Glass School. 1915. 14".*

Collection: Bernd Lienemann.

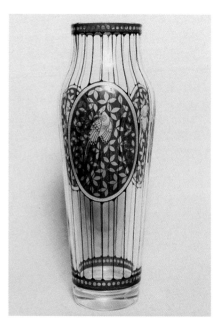

1	2
3	4

1: *Covered jar. Dark amethyst. Cut; acid etched design filled with gold; white enamel. Designed at the Glass School Kamenický Šenov. Executed by Hermann Eiselt. 1925. 7½".*
Collection: Private.

2: *Covered jar. Designed at the Glass School Kamenický Šenov. Marked: K.K.F-S.ST.; M; VE. 1915-20. 5".*
Photo: Jürgen Fischer.

3: *Covered jar. Oertel. Yellow stain; engraved. 1920s. 9¼".*
Collection: Oertel Museum.

4: *Covered jar. Designed at the Glass School Nový Bor. 1920. 10".*
Photo: Jürgen Fischer.

1500-1800

1
2
3 | 4

1: *Bowl. Loetz. Designed by Dagobert Peche? ≈1920. 6".*
Collection: Private.

2: *Bowl. Designed at the Kamenický Šenov Glass School. Marked: J.E. Paper label: St.St. 1920s. 5¼".*
Collection: Glass Museum Kamenický Šenov.

3: *Bowl. Clear glass, stained red and yellow; cut and engraved. Palda. 1930s. 14"D.*
Collection: Elaine Palda Swiler.

4: *Vase. Yellow stain and colored enamels. Cut. Designed, and possibly executed, at the Glass School Nový Bor. 1915. 8".*
Collection: Private.

1000-1200

900-1200

1: *Bowl. Designed at the Kamenický Šenov Glass School, by Prof. Lippert or Eiselt. 1934. 6".*
   Collection: Glass Museum Kamenický Šenov.

2: *Bowl. 3 designs; acid etched and painted. Designed at the Kamenický Šenov Glass School. 1930s. 5½".*
   Collection: Glass Museum Kamenický Šenov.

3: *Vase. Executed by Josef Krásný. 1930s. 9¼".*
   Collection: Česká Lipa District Museum.

4: *Vase. Executed by Eduard Ziml. 1930s. 7".*
   Collection: Česká Lipa District Museum.

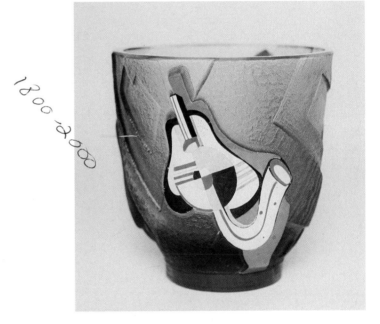

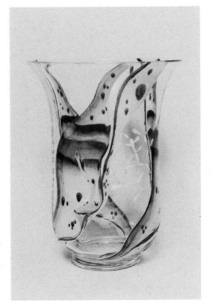

1 - 2	
3 - 4	
5 - 7	8-10

Vases with desert scenes. Similar decorations are pictured in both Hosch and Palda catalogs from the 1930s.

All are marked: Made in Czechoslovakia.

1: 8¼".
2: 10¼".
3: 10½".
4: 10½".
5: 10½".
6: 5¼".
7: 8¼".
8: 10¼".
9: 10¼".
10: 10¼".

All from the collection of Joe Mattis.

$$\frac{1 - 2}{3 - 4}$$
$$\frac{5 \mid 6}{}$$

1: *Pitcher. Crackle glass. Palda.
1930s. 7¾".*
Collection: Elaine Palda Swiler.

2: *Glass. Painted to simulate a
crackle finish. Palda. 1930s.
3¾".*
Collection: Elaine Palda Swiler.

3-4: *Glasses. Marked: MADE IN
CZECHO-SLOVAKIA. 1930s.
3".*
Collection: Ken Donmoyer.

5: *Covered vase. Palda. Product
#16387. 1930s. 12½".*
Collection: Česká Lipa District
Museum.

6: *Vase. Polished gold and black
enamel. Muhlhaus. ≈1935. 9¼".*
Collection: Private.

$$\frac{1 \text{ - } 2}{\begin{array}{c} 3 \text{ - } 6 \\ \hline 7 \mid 8 \end{array}}$$

1-2: *Vase and bowl. 1930s. 6½";*
2¼".
Collection: Joe Mattis.

3: *Vase. 1930s. 10".*
Collection: Charles and Barbara Plummer.

4: *Vase. 1930s. 8".*
Collection: Charles and Barbara Plummer.

5: *Vase. 1930s. 5".*
Collection: Charles and Barbara Plummer.

6: *Vase. 1930s. 6½".*
Collection: Charles and Barbara Plummer.

7: *Lamp. Marked: BELLOVA Czechoslovakia 2165. 1930s. 9¾".*
Collection: Joe Mattis.

8: *Lamp. 1930s. 11½".*
Collection: Joe Mattis.

Painted lamps were a staple item for the Nový Bor refineries.

Page 109:
Four pages from a Palda catalog, circa 1935.

Pages 110-111:
Four pages from a Rückl catalog of the same period.

TAFEL No. 1

B 5/241 — B 114/242 — B 81/8 — B 81/251 — B 81/252 — B 81/253 — B 112/248 — B 112/249

B 175/246 — B 175/243 — B 174/244 — B 1/56 — B 1/62 — B 2/60 — B 2/54 — B 99/155 — B 99/101 — B 82/22

B 70/140 — B 3/23 — B 3/91 — B 3/82 — B 3/69 — B 10/24 — B 10/83 — B 10/70 — B 69/20

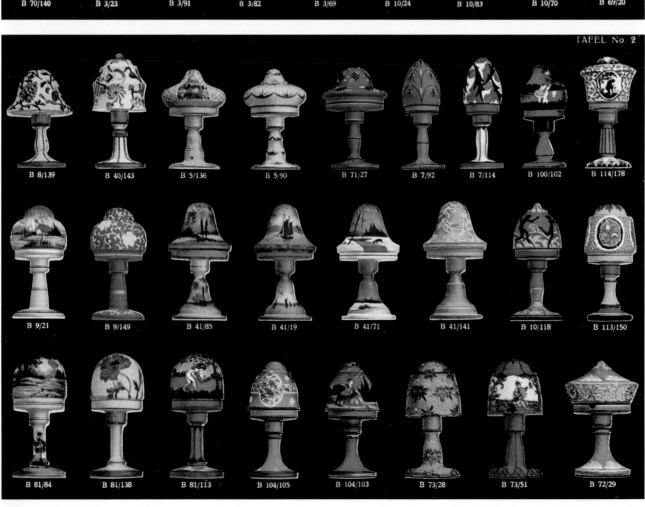

TAFEL No. 2

B 8/139 — B 40/143 — B 5/136 — B 5/90 — B 71/27 — B 7/92 — B 7/114 — B 100/102 — B 114/178

B 9/21 — B 9/149 — B 41/85 — B 41/19 — B 41/71 — B 41/141 — B 10/118 — B 113/150

B 81/84 — B 81/138 — B 81/113 — B 104/105 — B 104/103 — B 73/28 — B 73/51 — B 72/29

TAFEL No. 3

B 82/86   B 82/154   B 111/81   B 111/144   B 3/153   B 3/53   B 71/87   B 172/188   B 40/142   B 74/107

B 112/137   B 14/1   B 14/95   B 14/18   B 14/204   B 14/117   B 14/205   B 14/148

B 15/203   B 15/115   B 42/30   B 42/31   B 42/32   B 42/33   B 42/89

TAFEL No. 4

B 1/217   B 1/183   B 70/55   B 70/20   B 3/215   B 3/46   B 176/220   B 4/207   B 4/152   B 7/179

B 10/45   B 40/50   B 73/49   B 73/206   B 73/177   B 81/201   B 81/216   B 74/20

B 74/47   B 74/48   B 74/217   B 99/108   B 100/109   B 104/110   B 4/181   B 3/2   B 40/1

Only a small percentage of 20th century Bohemian glass has been well documented, making it easily identifiable. Identifying the vast majority of the Bohemian glass production is at best an educated guess. The glass produced from 1915 to 1945 has its own particular variety of problems.

Prior to the advent of the studio glass movement in the 1950s, the Czech glass industry was 90% market-driven. Both luxury and household glass were designed and produced with an end market in mind. If a market existed, the glass would be made. That encompassed the newest fashions as well as the historical models for which there was still a demand. A fairly large amount of Biedermeier and Second Rococo glass was produced in the 1920s and 1930s, as well as a generous amount of "brilliant cut" lead glass.

The rapidly growing interest in 20th century Bohemian glass gives rise to multiple opportunities for mis-attribution and questionable dating. The least harmful mistake a collector might make in regard to identification, is to attribute a piece of Bavarian or Silesian glass to a Bohemian firm. The Bavarian glassworks operated on the same principles as their Bohemian brethren. Their market strategy was similar, their glass schools were nearly identical, and they often employed the same independent designers. Bruno Mauder, the Director of the Glass School in Zwiesel (Bavaria), was very much in agreement with Josef Hoffmann of the Wiener Werkstätte and paralleled Hoffmann's designs, right down to the choice of colors. Alexander Pfohl, Jr. was the art director for Josephinenhütte in Silesia prior to teaching at the Glass School in Nový Bor. Almost every large collection of Bohemian glass will inadvertently include a few Bavarian and Silesian pieces.

Of greater concern to the collector is the glassware made since 1945 that is intended to be copies of older glass. A good deal of "between the wars" glass is still being produced -- not just in the Czech Republic, but in other eastern European countries, as well as in Asia.

The Egermann line of stained glass with engraved forest scenes has been in constant production for more than 160 years and has not changed a great deal in all that time. Numerous other Bohemian innovations have spanned the 20th century and have remained popular through many stylistic changes.

The glass we are able to show here represents the most readily available and most popular designs originating in the 1920s and 1930s.

RECENT AND CONTINUING PRODUCTION

```
  1 - 3
   4
 5 | 6 | 7
```

1-3: Egermann style glasses. Red stain; engraved. Currently produced by Exbor. 4½" - 7".
Studio Exbor.

All the "Pen Sketch" shown here was first produced by J.M.Pohl in the 1930s. The German word for pen sketch or pen and ink drawing is Federzeichnung. It is often used today to describe this type of painting and the fine gold tracery found on Lištované and similar glass.

4: Pen sketch footed bowl. Cranberry glass, with polished gold and black enamel. Currently produced by Exbor. 9".
Studio Exbor.

5: Pen sketch decanter. Cranberry glass over clear, with polished gold and black enamel. Currently produced by Exbor. 10½".
Studio Exbor.

6: Pen sketch vase. Amber glass with polished gold and black enamel. Cut. Currently produced by Exbor. 8".
Studio Exbor.

7: Pen sketch vase. Amber glass with polished gold and black enamel. Cut. Currently produced by Exbor. 9".
Studio Exbor.

These 6 pages showing Lištované are from a Crystalex catalog printed in the early 1970s.

Lištované was a natural evolution of "cut to clear" glass of the 19th century. However, it was unique enough to receive a patent around 1902 for Franz Heide of Česka Kamenice. Some Lištované predating 1940 can be found (Palda glass on p.19), but the vast majority of what is available has been made since 1960.

Most Lištované is made of overlay glass, laboriously cut and painted, although some pressed glass with colored stain simulating cut panels can be found.

```
     1 - 3
     4 - 5
 6 | 7-8 | 9
```

1-3: *Lištované decanter and wine glasses. Blue over clear. Silver tracery. Currently produced by Exbor. 4¼"; 11½"; 7¼".*
Studio Exbor.

4-5: *Lištované wine glasses. Blue over clear. Gold tracery. Currently produced by Jílek Brothers. 8¼".*
Collection: Private.

6: *Perfume. Pressed and polished; pressed stopper. Currently produced in Japan. Paper label: Irice. 4¼".*
Collection: Private.

7-8: *Pitcher and glass. Red cut to clear. Made in Romania and imported in the early 1970s by A. A. Imports. 10"; 4".*
Collection: Private.

9: *Amber vase with frieze of hunters and bears. Produced around 1950 from a pre-war design. 10".*
Collection: Private.

1	
2 - 3	
4 - 6	7
8	

1: Smoke Topaz vase. Broad facet cut with frieze of Amazon warriors. Currently produced by Moser. 9¾".
Collection: Private.

2: Rosalin vase. Broad facet cut. Currently produced by Moser. 11¼".
Collection: Private.

3: Royalit vase. Broad facet cut with frieze of Amazon warriors. Currently produced by Moser. 8¾".
Collection: Private.

4-6: Decanter and glasses. "Rose" decoration. Engraved; gilt. Moser. From 1902 -present. 5¼"; 14½".
Collection: Private.

7: Frieze showing Amazon warriors. From vase #3 on this page. Produced by Moser in the 1980s.

8: Frieze showing Amazon warriors. From the vase shown on page 29. Produced by Moser in the 1920s.

The acid etched friezes currently produced by Moser closely resemble those of the 1920s. For the most part, the background of the earlier friezes appears as a green/brown patina.

$$\frac{1}{\begin{array}{c}2 - 4\\ \hline 5\text{-}6 \mid 7\end{array}}$$

1: Bowl. Frosted glass with purple threads and prunts. Currently produced by Von Poschinger in Frauneau, Germany. 8" wide.
Collection: Private.

2-3: "Ingrid" vase and ash tray. Green malachite. Pressed. Currently produced by Ornela from the original Schlevogt molds. 4½"H; 4¾"W.
Collection: Irma and Richard Hosch.

4: "Ingrid" ash tray. Green malachite. Pressed. Currently produced by either Ornela or Jižerský Sklo in Jablonec. 3".
Collection: Irma and Richard Hosch.

"INGRID" PRODUCTION
Prior to the restitution of property in 1990, all of the molds belonging to Hoffmann and Schlevogt were kept in the former Riedel glassworks in Desna. This glassworks (now Ornela) had exclusive use of the Hoffmann and Schlevogt molds. After 1990, a small number of molds were given to other private firms, most notably Jižerský Sklo in Jablonec.

One often finds this type of glass with fraudulent marks, such as Lalique, Moser, and even Steuben.

5-6: Figurines. "Dancer" and "Girl in the Wind." Frosted glass designed in the early 1930s by Schwetz-Lehmann for Schlevogt. Both currently produced by Ornela. 8½".
Collection: Private.

7: "Ingrid" vase. Amethyst. 4 women with draped clothes. Pressed. Produced in the 1950s and '60s in amethyst, green and clear frosted glass. (Only malachite is an original color.) 10".
Collection: Private.

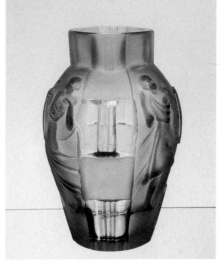

$$\frac{1}{\frac{2 - 5}{6 - 7 \mid 8}}$$

1: *"Diana, the Huntress." Originally produced by the Bimini Werkstätte in Vienna and the Glass School at Železný Brod. Currently produced by Železný Brod Sklo. 10".*
Collection: Private.

2-5: *Železný Brod figurines made from solid rods. Whimsical animal figurines made by Železný Brod Sklo and numerous small shops in the Železný Brod area; also made in Germany, Bulgaria and Poland. 2½" to 3½".*
Collection: Private.

6-7: *Storks. Blown from solid rod by a lampworker. Made in the Železný Brod area; similar work is done throughout central Europe. Left is 3½"; Right is 5½".*
Collection: Private.

8: *Dentist. Part of the Doctor series originating in the 1970s. Made at Železný Brod Sklo. Solid glass made "at the furnace." 8".*
Collection: Joe and Susan Milzman.

THE GLASS INDUSTRY 1939-1945

The Munich Accord of September 29, 1938 ceded the forest areas surrounding most of Czechoslovakia – the Sudetenland – to Germany. Under the disguise of protecting the German-speaking population of the border areas, the German army was allowed to occupy the Sudetenland and gain a large percentage of the Czech manufacturing base as well as the mineral producing areas, especially the coal mines. Following this successful ploy by Germany, Poland and Hungary attempted to do much the same. Hitler moved quickly to prevent any further border changes and effectively took control of all of Czechoslovakia in March 1939.

Glass production was deemed a vital industry by the occupying government and since the industry was in the hands of the German-speaking Bohemians, only minor changes occurred in 1939. As German aggression grew into World War II, the entire nomenclature of the glass industry changed. Exports were limited to those countries that were easily accessible and were either friendly to or controlled by Germany. From the limited amount of surviving records, we can glean a picture of an industry surviving on sheer determination, although shortages of every kind limited production to the bare essentials. Even so, people had to eat. If you were a glassblower or a glass painter, that is how you survived.

Sufficient records are available concerning the major producers and their activities, to give us some idea of the types of glass produced during World War II. The Glass Schools continued to train students and to provide new designs. The firms of Goldberg, Hosch, and Oertel (and many others) supplied plain and some forms of luxury glass during the war years, mostly for the interior and German markets. The glass manufacturers were hard pressed to keep their furnaces fired. Many were forced to shut down and the glass blowers worked on a rotating basis, going from plant to plant, seldom working more than one day a week.

One notable exception to the crisis was the Moser glass works at Karlovy Vary. Leo Moser left the firm in September 1932, leaving the bankrupt company in the hands of the Czechoslovak Union Bank. The company slowly regained some of its profitability, and by 1935 was exporting to more than 25 countries. At the Exhibition in Brussels in 1935, the Moser firm won a Grand Prize for its cut glass and vivid colors, and another at the 7th Trienale in Milan in 1940. Throughout the war years, exhibitions continued to be held and the Moser firm – renamed the "Staatliche Glasmanufaktur Karlsbad A.G." in 1941 – became the flagship for Bohemian glass.

The renamed company was awarded the same status as the prestigious Berlin porcelain manufacturer (Staatliche Porzellanmanufaktur Berlin) and the director of the porcelain company, Max Pfeiffer, was appointed director of the glass firm. Under these conditions, the Karlovy Vary glass house was assured at least the minimum materials needed to keep operating at an artistic level and to participate in various exhibitions -- Zurich in 1943 and Prague in 1944. Designers during this era included W. Wagenfeld, T. Petri, and S. Schütz. Many of the earlier designs by Josef Hoffmann were recreated or modified. Despite the war-time hardships, people in many parts of Germany and central Europe maintained a pre-war life style until the tide turned in 1943.

In 1945, when the Beneš government returned, it immediately began the process of nationalization, starting with firms of 50 or more employees. Within a year, all firms had been taken over by the government and run by various political committees. Although nationalized, most of the firms continued to use their pre-war names until 1948.

Fate was less kind to the firm Johan Loetz Witwe in Klášterský Mlýn. It suffered a fate similar to that of the Moser firm, except there was to be no salvation for this once proud firm. Bankrupt, devastated by fire, and out of the hands of the Spaun family, the factory was leased by Paul Beate from Spieglau, Germany in 1939. Beate produced common household glass for the interior and Bavarian markets. In 1942, ownership was transferred to Julius Altmann-Althausen from Bucharest, who continued to produce household glass until the firm was nationalized. In 1948, the factory was deemed unnecessary and was torn down. The former residence of the Spaun family, designed by Leopold Bauer, was converted to a multi-family apartment house, which is still in use.

There can be no doubt that the Czech people suffered greatly under the Nazi regime, but the indomitable spirit of the 600 year old glass industry found ways to deal with this crisis as it had done many times before. Even in the worst of times, someone in Bohemia is working at making glass.

The mere mention of the word Bohemia conjures up an image of Camelot, except that Bohemia is an area with well-defined, albeit changing, borders. Over the centuries, the area increased and decreased, particularly the eastern borders, with the political fortunes of the times. The map on page 121 shows a fairly good approximation of the shape of Bohemia in the 1920s and '30s. It is an area of about 20,100 square miles (about 4,000 square miles smaller than West Virginia).

The glass industry in particular has clung to the identity of being Bohemian through many political changes. If a man had been born in his family home in Nový Bor in 1917, he would have been born in Austria. From 1918 to 1938, he would have lived in Czechoslovakia. From 1938 to 1945, he lived in Germany. From 1945 to 1993, he was back in Czechoslovakia. And if he died in 1994, he would have been buried in the Czech Republic. All of that without ever leaving his home town. If you inquired about his nationality, he would most likely tell you "I am Bohemian."

The glass making and refining industry was concentrated in the forest areas , stretching from the northeast, westward to the south. By the era of alternate fuels (other than wood) certain areas were firmly established as glass producing. The glass refiners were often located in the proximity of the glass makers (shaded areas on the map), especially the glass cutters. The painters and engravers were heavily concentrated in the north eastern portion of Bohemia (from Kamenický Šenov to Jablonec), necessitating a fair amount of shipping. Several glass makers were located close to Nový Bor but, in the town itself there was only one glass maker, Hantich (Florahütte).

In any given year from 1870 to 1945, there were about 100 glass houses producing a variety of products ranging from window glass to the highest forms of art glass. In 1930, a reasonably good year for production, there were just over 62,000 people employed in the glass industry. As the great depression took its toll, followed by World War II, the industry was severely tested. The years following 1945 reveal their own contributions and detractions, and that will be the subject of *Collectible Bohemian Glass, Volume 3.*

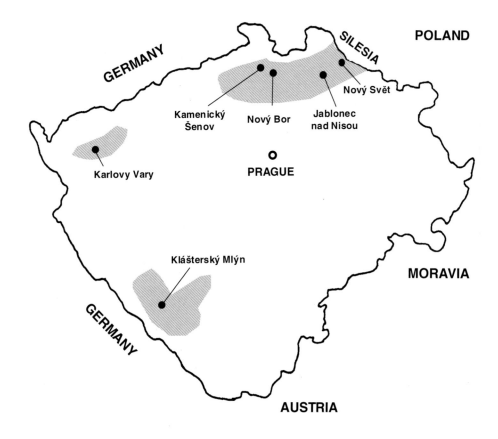

Bohemia — 1920s and 1930s

Statistically speaking, most Bohemian glassware is not marked or signed in a permanent manner. There are instances, however, when a piece will be found with an artist's or designer's name or initials, and occasionally an original label is still intact. Those features add to the enjoyment of the piece and help to put it into its historic perspective.

"Marked" pieces typically have the word Czechoslovakia acid etched, sand blasted, or enamel transferred on the bottom, or a label will show only "Made in Czechoslovakia" or "Austria." Pressed glass might have the word Czechoslovakia cut into the mold and, in the case of Heinrich Hoffmann's pressed glass, a trademark butterfly is often included in the mold.

"Signed" pieces are usually signed in a manner consistent with the refinement. Engraved glass will have the initials engraved, whereas painted glass will be signed in enamel. When a full name is written out, it is typically done with a diamond scribe. Cameo glass is usually signed by acid etching the firm's name somewhere within the decoration. The term "marked" can refer to any identifying mark, whereas "signed" should be used only when it identifies a particular company or person.

The Moser firm has thoroughly searched its archives for all of the marks and signatures ever used by the firm and has published them in a catalog of an exhibit commemorating its 140th year. The firm has given us permission to reproduce this information (pages 126-128) and we are sure it will be helpful to collectors. Undoubtedly other authentic Moser markings are found on an isolated example, but the official Moser reference is the most accurate available source of marks to date.

Another good source of information is the 1006 page "*Glasmarken Lexikon, 1600-1945*" (Encyclopedia of Glass Marks) written by Carolus Hartmann and published by Arnoldsche in 1997.

The various marks "Made in Czechoslovakia" or "Czechoslovakia" found in numerous variations, were not registered to any specific company according to the archivists in Cheb and Liberec. Two marks do consistently appear on glassware by a known maker, however. The firm Loetz Witwe is known to use the oval mark (shown as Mark #1 on page 123) consistently on its glass, and the mark has not been found on the glassware of any other maker. The other mark on page 123 is quite distinct and has often been found on the glass produced by the firm of Wilhelm Kralik. Kralik's glass is not as well documented as that of Loetz, so it is possible that this mark has been used by other firms, and that Kralik used additional marks. For purposes of speculation, one could say that Mark #1 on a piece of glass indicates at least a 90% probability that it was made by the Loetz

MARKS, SIGNATURES AND MONOGRAMS

firm. Mark #2 would indicate a 60-70% probability that the glass was made by the Kralik firm. The remaining variations may never be sorted out.

Fortunately, many individuals and companies used their full name on their glassware and it leaves the collector only to read what has been written. All too often we must deal with initials only; sometimes straightforward, often in some form of monogram. If initials are present, someone only has to refer to the index in this or other books to find a probable match. If the initials are in the form of a monogram, the problem is more acute.

Page 124 shows the monograms used by some of the best known designers and artists working between the years 1910 and 1945. In some cases, the mark can constitute positive identification -- if it is distinct and exclusive to that particular producer. In many other instances, the marks are so similar that further research is required. For example, the monograms for Lotte Baar and Leopold Bauer can easily be interchanged.

The Wiener Werkstätte monogram shown was used on glass designed by the Werkstätte for Moser. Several other variations of the letters WW were used by other producers and by the Werstätte artists. Also, there were unrelated artists with the initials WW, such as Wilhelm Wagenfeld and Winkler and Wittig of Nový Bor.

The monograms shown on page 124 were hand drawn from the glass pictured in this book or from some reliable source, such as:
· *Glaskunst der Moderne*, Bröhan, 1992.
· *Das Böhmische Glas*, Passau Glass Museum, 1995.
· *Moser 1857-1997*, Moser, 1997.
· *New Glass Review*, Prague.

Mark #1. Attributed to Loetz.   Mark # 2. Attributed to Kralik.

INDIVIDUALS

 Baar, Lotte

 Bauer, Leopold

 Bayerl, Bernhardine

 Beckert, Adolf

 Beckert, Adolf

 Bischof, August

 Eiselt, Arnold

 Eiselt, Paul

 Helzel, August

 Helzel, Ernst

 Horn, Richard

 Hussmann, Heinrich

 Kirschner, Marie

 Kreibich, Gustav

 Kromer, Emil

 Moser, Koloman

 Paulin, Ida

 Peche, Dagobert

 Pfohl, Erwin

 Pfohl, Erwin

 Pietsch, Otto (Jr.)

 Pietsch, Otto (Sr.)

 Powolny, Michael

 Přenosil, Ladislav

 Prutscher, Otto

 Rossler, Max

 Rossler, Max

 Tauschek, Otto

 Zadikow, Arnold

 Zeh, Hermann

FIRMS

 Conrath & Liebsch

 Goldberg (Carl)

 Lobmeyr, J & L

 Meyr's Neff

 Moser

 Oertel

 Oertel

 Oertel

 Rasche (Adolf)

 J. Schreiber & Neffen

 Wiener Werkstätte

 Wünsch (Carl)

The Glass Schools in Kamenický Šenov, Nový Bor, and Železný Brod contributed many designs to the Bohemian manufacturers and refiners. The Glass Schools were not in the business of refining glass for profit. At various exhibits, however, they would sell a few items. Those items would bear the initials or the label from the school. Glass that was kept in the school's collection would also be appropriately labeled or signed.

We photographed an unusually large number of signed pieces because those items were given to the various local museums by the Glass Schools.

Kamenický Šenov (Steinschönau)

K.K. F-S. ST.

Nový Bor (Haida)

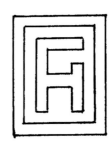

Železný Brod (Eisenbrod)

S.Š. 127/32 ŽB

The initials in the marks help indicate the time period, with some small amount of overlap. Prior to 1918, the schools used K.K. for Königlich und Kaiserlich (royal and imperial). F.S. stands for Fachschule. After 1918, K.K. was replaced by S.F. for Staatfachschule (state technical school).

The Železny Brod School used the letters S.Š. for Sklárské Škole (glass school). If signed, glass from the Železný Brod School was usually signed on the bottom with the form number and the date. Some times the professor's or student's initials would also be included.

These three pages of registered trademarks and company marks are reprinted from
Moser 1857-1997 with permission of the Moser company.

no.	graphic or textual form	period of use or validity of the mark	date of registration, notes	execution
1		approx. 1880		sticker with black print
2	*MOSER*	approx. 1880 - 1893		written in gold or colour
3		approx. 1880 - 1890		sticker with black print
4	*Moser*	approx. 1880 - 1890		engraved
5		1898 - 1918	Registered at OŽK Cheb, December 31, 1898 (no. 631) its use is documented even before its registration with various inscriptions - MOSER; MADE IN AUSTRIA; MOSER AUSTRIA;	sticker with black print coloured stamp
6	MK	1911 - 1938	Registered at OŽK Cheb, June 14, 1911 (no. 1987)	acid-etched
7	*Moser Karlsbad*	1911 - 1938	Registered at OŽK Cheb, June 14, 1911 (no. 1987) its use is documented even before its registration in the 1920s generally complemented by the inscription: "Made in Czecho Slovakia" in some cases "Made in Čecho Slovakia" engraved	engraved acid-etched stamp with acid-etched tincture coloured stamp written in gold
	Orogravure	1919 - 1929	Registered at OŽK Cheb, April 15, 1919 (no. 2976)	text
	Oroplastique	1919 - to the present	Registered at OŽK Cheb, April 15, 1919 (no. 2977)	text
8		1919 - 1938	Registered at OŽK Cheb, December 13, 1919 (no. 5523)	sticker with black print coloured stamp
9		approx. 1910 - 1925	unregistered combination of marks numbers 6, 7, 8 used as a company sticker	sticker with brown print
10		1923 - 1933	Registered at OŽK Cheb, March 9, 1923 (no. 3846)	acid-etched coloured stamp
	Verroplastik	1924 - 1934	Registered at OŽK Cheb; February 14, 1924 (no. 4050)	text
	Oropantogravur	1924 - 1934	Registered at OŽK Cheb, February 14, 1924 (no. 4051)	text

no.	graphic or textual form	period of use or validity of the mark	date of registration, notes	execution
	Animor	1925 - 1935	Registered at OŽK Cheb, August 30, 1926 (no. 4779)	text
11		1926 - 1936	Registered at OŽK Cheb, August 30, 1926 (no. 4780) used only as an advertising mark probably not used as mark on objects	
12		1926 - 1936	Registered at OŽK Cheb, December 9,. 1926 (no. 4851)	sticker with black print
13		approx. 1926 - 1930	unregistered variation no. 12	acid-etched
14		approx. 1926 - 1950	unregistered variation no. 12	engraved used until the present as engraved mark stamp with acid-etched tincture coloured stamp
15		approx. 1926 - 1936	unregistered variation no. 12	stamp with acid-etched tincture
16		approx. 1928 - 1930	unregistered variation no. 6	stamp with acid-etched tincture
	Acidoplastik	1928 - 1938	Registered at OŽK Cheb, February 12,1928 (no. 5067)	text
	Argentoplastik	1928 - 1938	Registered at OŽK Cheb, February 12, 1928 (no. 5068)	text
	Patinor	1928 - 1938	Registered at OŽK Cheb, February 12, 1928 (no. 5069)	text
17		1929 - to the present	Registered at OŽK Cheb, January 31, 1929 (no. 5341)	stamp with acid-etched tincture
	Gipsy Gläser	1929 - 1939	Registered at OŽK Cheb, May 31, 1929 (no. 5428)	text
18		1929 - to the present	Registered at OŽK Cheb, June 27, 1929 (no. 5453)	stamp with acid-etched tincture
19		1929 - to the present	Registered at OŽK Cheb, June 27, 1929 (no. 5454)	stamp with acid-etched tincture
20		1930 - to the present	Registered at OŽK Cheb, August 16, 1930 (no. 5725)	stamp with acid-etched tincture
21		1932 - to the present	Registered at OŽK Cheb, February 17, 1932 (no. 6135)	stamp with acid-etched tincture

no.	graphic or textual form	period of use or validity of the mark	date of registration, notes	execution
22		1936 - to the present	Z: OŽK Cheb, 1. 9. 1936 (č. 7641)	stamp with acid-etched tincture
23		1936 - 1938	unregistered variation no. 22	stamp with acid-etched tincture coloured stamp
24		1941 - 1945		engraved
25		1946 - to the present	Czech variation of the old mark Moser Karlsbad, OŽK Cheb March 28, 1946 (no. 8417)	stamp with acid-etched tincture
26		approx. 1950 - to the present	unregistered variation no. 13 used as a sticker probably until the 1960s	sticker, yellow print on silver - to the background stamp with acid-etched tincture
27		approx. 1960 - 1970	unregistered variation no. 26	sticker, yellow print on gold background
28		1957	unregistered variation no. 26 used on the occasion of the 100th anniversary of the firm's founding	sticker, violet print on silver background
		1960 - to the present	Registered on December 31, 1960 (no. 154808) mark of the Giant Snifters Club designed by F. Chocholatý, September 17, 1960 on the certificate presented to the club members	
29		1962	unregistered variation no. 26 used on the occasion of the 105th anniversary of the firm's founding	sticker, dark blue print on silver background
30		1966 - to the present	Registered on 25. 3. 1966 (no. 157018) on January 11, 1996 inscription changed to CZECH REPUBLIC	sticker, black print on gold background
31		1970s and 1980s	unregistered variation no. 26	sticker, black print on gold background
32		1970s and 1980s	unregistered variation no. 26	sticker, black and red print on gold background
33		1992 - to the present	Registered on April at 16, 1992 (no. 170410)	textual mark in different forms after 1995 sand-blasted
34		1991 - 1992	unregistered variation no. 33	sticker, wine-red print on gold background
35		1996 - to the present	unregistered variation no. 33 used for designers' works of the Moser Studio	sand-blasted

VALUE GUIDE

This information is presented both as a study in economics and philosophy. Our opinions are the results of ten years of collecting Bohemian glass and doing enough research to produce three books. The availability of the Internet and access to worldwide sales, plus the numerous antique shows we attend, have given us a good deal of information that we have drawn upon for the values presented here. It remains, however, our opinions, and can only be useful to the reader when used with other criteria.

The value of a piece of glass is not the same as the price. Prices fluctuate widely, with the economy, the locality, and the profit the seller hopes to realize.

Even if every seller could buy glass at the same wholesale price, the cost of doing business varies greatly from shop to shop. If you choose to purchase a particular vase from a shop on Rodeo Drive or 5th Avenue, it stands to reason that you could buy that same vase at a country auction for considerably less. While there are many good reasons to patronize the high profile shops, low price is not one of them.

Values, on the other hand, tend to be more stable and depend on each particular item to speak for itself. Selling prices typically reflect the current interest in any given item. Value is more reflective of long term stability. Remember Avon bottles?

Values and prices have many common factors that determine the ultimate dollar amount. Demand and availability are two recognized factors for setting the selling (asking) price and they have a genuine bearing on the true dollar value of the piece. Rare and unusual pieces are worth more and cost more. Period.

This does not address the personal value that an individual might place on a particular item. Sentimental value adds nothing to the worth of an item. Grandmother's wedding present can only be judged for what it is. This does not mean that personal value is not important. An object that can give you pleasure on a daily basis is certainly valuable and most people will gladly pay something extra for such an object.

Many antique dealers, especially those specializing in glass, are able to sell things for their true value or at least close to it, due to their skill and knowledge in acquiring their inventory.

The values shown here are for the **specific** pieces of glass illustrated. Very often, **similar** looking glass can be worth considerably more or less than the item illustrated.

There is no substitute for comparative shopping.

We have asked numerous collectors and dealers how they define value and price. Basically they all agree that:

1) Price is what you pay. Value is what is left after you subtract the seller's markup, sales talk, and embellishments.

2) Price is what you pay. Value is what you could sell it for.

THINGS THAT *DO* ADD VALUE

Authentic signatures and dates.
Well publicized pieces.
Absolute confirmation of manufacturer or refiner.
Scarcity (shape, decoration, color).
Condition.
Awarded a prize at an exhibition.
Similar pieces in a museum or prominent collection.

THINGS THAT *DO NOT* ADD VALUE

False or erroneous attribution or information.
Previous ownership.
Seller's overhead and profit margin.
Short term demand.
Forms and decorations that are out of character for the producer.

This value guide is based upon the market for the years 1997 and 1998. It relies heavily on auction prices and show prices where the dealer is moving mechandise at a reasonable pace. In the end, however, only the buyer and seller can determine what will be paid.

CUT GLASS

PAGE 10
1-2	$100-150 pair
3, 5	$ 60-75 each
4	$150-200
6	$100-150
7-8	$200-250 pair

PAGE 14
1, 3	$ 50-75 each
2	$200-250
4, 6	$ 50-75 each
5	$200-250
7, 9	$ 50-75 each
8	$200-250
10,12	$ 50-75 each
11	$200-250

PAGE 17
1-10	$150-200 each

PAGE 18
2-3	$300-400 each
4	$150-200
5	$200-250
6	$300-350
7	$350-400

PAGE 19
1	$450-600
2	$500-650
3-5	$200-250 each
6	$400-550
7	$300-400
8	$350-450

PAGE 20
1, 2	$500-600
3	$400-500
4	$500-650
5-6	$350-400 each
7	$400-500

PAGE 21
1	$400-500
2	$450-550
3	$500-600

PAGE 22
1	$550-700
2	$350-450
3	$300-350
4	$500-600

PAGE 23
1	$400-600
2	$500-700
3, 4	$400-600
5	$400-500
6	$350-450
7	$300-400

PAGE 24
1	$350-500
2	$700-900
3	$100-150
4	$ 50-75
5	$150-250
6	$300-400
7	$250-300
8	$200-300

PAGE 25
1	$450-600
2	$500-750
3	$300-400
4	$450-600
5	$300-350
6	$350-450

PAGE 26
1	$3000-3500
2	$1500-1800
3	$ 900-1200
4	$ 750-850
5	$1200-1400
6	$ 250-300
7	$ 750-850

PAGE 27
1	$2000-2500
2	$1600-1800
3	$1500-2000
4	$3000-3500
5	$ 300-450
6	$ 500-600

PAGE 28
1	$ 500-650
2	$ 450-600
3	$3000-3500
4	$4000-5000
5	$ 800-1000
6	$2000-2500

PAGE 29
1	$1500-2000
2	$1500-2000
3	$ 300-350
4	$ 500-600
5	$1000-1200
6	$ 850-1000
7	$ 550-700
8	$1500-1800

PAGE 30
1	$ 800-1200
2	$ 900-1200
3	$1000-1400
4	$ 800-1000

PAGE 31
1	$2000-2500
2	$1500-1800
3	$1200-1500
4	$ 400-500
5	$ 300-350
6	$ 300-400

ENGRAVED GLASS

PAGE 33
1-3	$900-1200
4-6	$900-1200

PAGE 34
1-4	$3000-4000
5-6	$1200-1500

PAGE 35
1	$ 250-300
2	$2000-2500
3	$2500-3000
4	$ 250-300
5	$ 400-550

PAGE 36
1-2	$1500-2000
3-4	$2500-3000

PAGES 37-45
Drahoňovský: The type of engraved glass shown here has no current history of selling prices; however, the rarity of the pieces would indicate values in the $3000 to $5000 price range.

FURNACE DECORATED GLASS

PAGE 48
1-5	$125-175 each
6-8	$125-150 each
9-13	$125-200 each

PAGE 49
1-9	$125-175 each

PAGE 50
1-4	$250-300 each
5	$450-600
6	$300-350
7	$350-400

PAGE 51

1	$ 400-500
2	$ 300-350
3	$ 300-350
4	$ 400-500
5	$3000-4000
6	$ 300-350
7	$ 350-400

PAGE 52

1-3	$200-300 each
4	$200-250
5	$150-175
6	$300-350
7	$150-200

PAGE 53

1-4	$250-300 each
5-8	$300-350 each

PAGE 54

1-9	$250-300 each

PAGE 55

1-2	$400-500 each
3-5	$150-200 each
6-8	$125-175 each

PAGE 56

1-4	$175-250 each
5-7	$250-300 each
8-10	$150-175 each

PAGE 57

1-3	$200-250 each
4-7	$125-200 each
8-10	$125-175 each
11-13	$225-300 each

PAGE 58

1-5	$175-250 each
6-8	$225-275 each
9-10	$250-300 each
11-12	$150-200 each

PAGE 59

1-4	$175-250 each
5, 7	$150-200 pair
6	$150-200
8	$ 75-125
9-11	$175-250 each

PAGE 60

1-3	$175-250 each
4-5	$225-275 each
6-7	$150-200 each
8	$200-250

PAGE 61

1-4	$200-275 each
5	$150-200
6	$350-400
7	$150-175
8	$200-250

PAGE 62

1	$200-250
2	$150-200
3-5	$125-200 each
6-8	$125-150 each

PAGE 63

1-3	$175-225 each
4-11	$150-200 each

PAGE 64

1	$ 75-100
2	$125-175
3-4	$100-150 each
5	$150-200
6	$125-150
7	$250-300

PAGE 65

1	$600-750
2-3	$400-500
4	$500-650
5	$450-550

PAGE 66

1-2	$200-250 each
3-5	$150-250 each
6-7	$200-250 each

PAGE 67

1-2	$150-200 pair
3, 5	$150-200 pair
4	$175-250
6	$200-250
7	$100-150
8	$ 60-75
9	$175-225

PAGE 68

1	$225-275
2	$450-600
3	$225-275
4	$250-300

PAGE 69

1	$ 50-100
2	$225-300
3-4	$200-300
5-6	$250-300

PAGE 70

1, 3	$150-200 pair
2	$175-250
4, 6	$100-125 pair
5	$150-200
7-9	$ 35-50 each
10-11	$300-400 each

PAGE 71

1	$200-275
2-3	$300-400 each
4-5	$300-350 each

PAGE 72

1	$300-400
2-8	$125-175 each
9	$200-250

PAGE 73

1	$2500-3000
2	$3000-3500
3	$ 400-500
4	$ 500-600
5	$ 450-600
6	$ 350-500

PAGE 74

1	$1200-1500
2	$ 250-300
3-4	$ 150-200

PRESSED GLASS

PAGE 77

	$20-25 each

PAGE 78

1	$600-650
2	$250-300
3, 5	$ 20-30 each
4	$ 75-100
6-10	$ 25-50 each

PAGE 79

1	$300-400
2	$ 25-50 pair
3	$200-300
4	$ 50-75 each
5	$200-300

FIGURINES

PAGE 82

	$200-300

PAGE 83

1	$ 150-200
2	$1500-2000
3	$ 250-300
4	$ 350-400
5-7	$ 150-200 each

PAGE 84

1	$750-1000
2	$500-750
3	$300-350
4	$200-250
5	$250-350
6	$150-200

PAGE 85
1	$250-300
2	$300-400
3	$100-150
4-5	$175-250

PAINTED GLASS

PAGE 90
1	$ 450-500
2	$ 400-450
3	$ 800-1000
4-7	$2000-2500 each

PAGE 91
1	$ 600-750
2	$ 500-650
3	$ 300-400
4	$ 500-650
5	$1000-1200
6	$ 800-900

PAGE 92
1-2	$ 800-1200 each
3	$1000-1200
4	$1200-1400
5	$1200-1500
6	$1000-1200
7	$ 400-600

PAGE 93
1-2	$ 500-700 each
3-4	$ 200-300 each
5	$1000-1400
6	$ 800-1000
7	$1200-1500

PAGE 94
1	$1000-1200
2	$ 750-850
3-4	No appropriate value possible
5-7	$1000-1500

PAGE 95
1	$ 300-400
2	$1200-1500
3-4	No appropriate value possible
5	$1500-2000
6	$1200-1600

PAGE 96
1-2	$1200-1500 each
3	$ 300-400
4-5	$ 400-500 each
6-7	$1200-1500 each
8	$ 800-1000

PAGE 97
1	$200-300
2	$300-400
3	$ 75-125
4	$125-175
5-7	$150-200 each

PAGE 98
1	$ 200-250
2	$ 250-300
3	$ 750-1000
4	$ 500-600
5	$ 300-500
6	$1200-1500

PAGE 99
1	$ 400-600
2	$1500-2000
3	$ 150-200
4	$1800-2200

PAGE 100
1	$2000-2500
2	$1500-2000
3	$ 500-650
4	$ 500-600
5	$ 600-750

PAGE 101
1	$ 700-850
2	$ 600-750
3	$ 700-800
4	$ 350-400
5	$ 750-900
6	$1000-1500

PAGE 102
1	$450-700
2	$400-500
3	$500-800
4	$900-1200

PAGE 103
1	$ 500-750
2-3	$3000-3500
4	$1500-1800

PAGE 104
1	$1500-1800
2	$ 900-1200
3	$1000-1200
4	$ 900-1200

PAGE 105
1	$ 600-750
2	$1800-2000
3	$ 600-750
4	$ 350-450

PAGE 106
	$150-225 each

PAGE 107
1	$250-300
2	$ 50-65
3-4	$ 50-60 each
5	$500-650
6	$400-500

PAGE 108
1	$ 80-120
2	$ 75-100
3-4	$100-150 each
5	$ 75-125
6	$ 50-75
7	$750-1000
8	$250-300

RECENT AND CONTINUING PRODUCTION

The glassware shown in this section can be found in gift shops and department stores at varying prices. No. 9 on page 115 is no longer produced and has a value of $125-175.

INDEX